Just Enough French

Jacqueline Lecanuet & Ron Overy

Hugo's Language Books Limited

Also available in a pack with two cassettes, ISBN 0 85285 221 5

Written by
Jacqueline Lecanuet & Ron Overy
South Bank University

Edited by
Ruth Nason

Illustrations by Sonia Robinson

Set in Palatino and Optima by
Andrew Burrell

Printed and bound in Great Britain by
Scotprint

Other titles in this series
Just Enough German
Just Enough Italian
Just Enough Spanish
Just Enough Hindi

ACKNOWLEDGEMENTS
We want to say thank you to all those French people living
and working in St Lô in Normandy who kindly contributed to
this book. Thank you also to Jean Cooper for typing the
manuscript. And finally, a special "Merci" to my mother,
Hélène Lecanuet, for all her advice and encouragement.

Contents

Preface

Just Enough French forms part of a new series of short courses from Hugo, intended for busy people who want to learn just enough of a language to enable them to "cope" with most situations when they travel abroad.

In preparing **Just Enough French**, our aims have been:

1) to provide you with a basic, all-purpose vocabulary and a carefully chosen range of language patterns, sufficient to enable you to communicate in French in a simple, effective way;
2) to offer you interesting and occasionally humorous dialogues and practice sessions, designed to ensure that the right French words and structures will come to mind automatically when you need them;
3) to give you, with the help of audio cassettes and printed guidance, an excellent pronunciation, so that you can be understood immediately by French people.

Our philosophy throughout has been to teach "just enough", but to teach it well.

The opening chapter deals with pronunciation rules and then the following ten chapters all consist of:

1) Several **mini-dialogues** presented in French and English;
2) Relevant and useful background **Information** about life in France;
3) Short **Language Notes** explaining how French sentences are built up;
4) Some entertaining practice material, headed "**Your Turn**";
   (Please note that the exercises practise the language structures and vocabulary covered in the chapter concerned,

but also require you to look up some new words in the Mini-Dictionary at the back of the book.

The answers to the questions in the "Your Turn" sections are all found in the **Key** on pages 101–105.)

5) A **"Forget-me-not"** section, suggesting some ways of remembering French words by association;

6) A **Word List** of all the new words that have been introduced in the chapter.

We recommend that you use this book together with the **Just Enough French** audio cassettes. The French voices recorded there will serve as ideal models for you to imitate. However, the book can be used without the tapes, if you prefer.

We think you will enjoy **Just Enough French** and we would like to wish you good luck with your studies. **Bonne chance!** and **Bon courage!**

1 Practise Pronouncing!

French is a beautiful language to listen to, but it can be just a little difficult for English-speaking people to pronounce, which is why, in Chapters 2-4 of this book and in certain later places, we have used special imitated pronunciation to help you.

We suggest, in fact, that you look now at the notes on **Imitated Pronunciation** below and then GO STRAIGHT AWAY TO CHAPTER 2 and start joining in with the dialogues there. Later, you can come back and look more closely at the pronunciation rules set out for reference here.

IMITATED PRONUNCIATION

In Chapters 2, 3 and 4, we have not only given English translations of the French dialogues, but have also included in brackets after each French speech a simple pronunciation guide, like this:

> **Bonjour, Madame**. (Bong-joor, Mah-dahm.)
> **Voici mon billet. Et voici le billet de ma femme**. (Vwah-see mong bee-yay. Ay vwah-see ler bee-yay der mah fahm.)

All you need to do is to say each syllable in the pronunciation guide, as if it were part of an English word. But bear in mind the following:

ng	sounds like "ng" in "sing", "wrong"
er	sounds like "er" in "her"
y	sounds like "y" in "yes"
j	sounds like "s" in "measure"
ü	has no equivalent in English; round your lips and try to say "ee"; the result should be the exact sound represented by "ü" in the pronunciation guide
ah	sounds like the "ah" in "father", but shorter

NOW GO STRAIGHT AWAY TO CHAPTER 2!

Use the following notes for reference only, when you need.

FRENCH CONSONANTS

Pronounce all consonants (i.e. all letters except the vowels "a", "e", "i", "o" and "u") as in English, but remember the following:

c 1) Before "e" or "i", "c" sounds like English "ss": **ce** (*this*)
2) Otherwise "c" sounds like "k": **café** (*coffee*)

ç Always sounds like "ss": **ça** (*that*)

g 1) Before "e" or "i", "g" sounds like "s" in "treasure": **gîte** (*self-catering accommodation*)
2) Otherwise "g" sounds like "g" in "go": **glace** (*ice cream*)

h Is always silent

j Always sounds like "s" in "treasure": **je** (*I*)

r The French "r" is made at the back of the throat, as if gargling: **Paris**

ch Usually sounds like "sh": **je cherche** (*I'm looking for*)

qu Sounds like "k": **Qui?** (*Who?*)

Important: With the exception of "c", "f", "l" and "r", consonants are normally silent at the end of a word.

VOWELS

a Sounds like "a" in "father", but shorter: **là** (*there*)

e 1) In the middle of a syllable "e" sounds like "ai" in "fair": **mer** (*sea*)
2) At the end of a syllable "e" sounds like "er" in "her": **je** (*I*)
3) At the end of a word with more than one syllable "e" is silent: **tasse** (*cup*)

é Sounds like "ay" in "say": **arrivé** (*arrived*)

è, ê Both sound like "ai" in "fair": **père** (*father*), **fenêtre** (*window*)

i, y Both sound like "ee" in "meet": **il** (*he*)

o Sometimes like "o" in "not": **dormir** (*to sleep*)
Sometimes like "o" in "oh": **trop** (*too much*)

u This sound has no equivalent in English (but you hear it in Scotland). Try to say "ee" with rounded lips: **rue** (*street*)

COMBINATIONS OF VOWELS

ai, ei	Sound like "ai" in "fair": **faire** (*to do, make*)
au, eau	Sound like "oh": **cadeau** (*gift*)
eu, œu	Sound like "er" in "her": **neuf** (*nine*), **œuf** (*egg*)
oi	Sounds like "wah": **boire** (*to drink*)
ou	Sounds like "oo" in "boot": **roue** (*wheel*)

NASAL SOUNDS

When "m" or "n" follows a vowel, the result is a nasal sound:

om, on	Sound like "ong" in "song": **nom** (*name*), **non** (*no*)
am, an, em, en	These four combinations sound like "ahng", that is to say, like "an" in "can't": **enfant** (*child*)
im, in, aim, ain, eim, ein	These six combinations sound like "ang" in "sang", or like "an" in "van" pronounced through the nose: **vin** (*wine*), **faim** (*hunger*)
um, un	Sound like "ung" in "sung", but pronounce the "u" like "er" in "her", i.e. "erng": **parfum** (*perfume*), **un** (*one/a*)
ien	Sounds like "yang": **bien** (*well*)

LIQUID SOUNDS

il, ill	These combinations sound like "y" in "yes": **travail** (*work*), **soleil** (*sun*), **brouillard** (*fog*)
gn	Sounds like "ni" in "companion": **campagne** (*countryside*)

OTHER VARIATIONS

er	At the end of words with more than one syllable, "er" sounds like "ay" in "say": **arriver** (*to arrive*), **fumer** (*to smoke*)
ez	When at the end of a word, "ez" sounds like "ay": **fermez** (*close*)

LIAISON

The French like their language to flow smoothly and, when they speak, they link one word to another; this is called liaison. Here's an example:

un petit enfant (*a small child*)

When words are joined in this way,

s, x	Sound like "z": **vous êtes** (*you are*)
d	Sounds like "t": **vend -il**? (*does he sell?*)
f	Sounds like "v": **neuf heures** (*nine o'clock*)

THE ALPHABET IN FRENCH

Finally, when you are travelling, you most certainly will have to spell your name, so learn how to pronounce the letters of the alphabet in French as soon as you can. We are giving you the imitated pronunciation:

A	ah	**H**	ahsh	**O**	oh	**V**	vay
B	bay	**I**	ee	**P**	pay	**W**	doobler-vay
C	say	**J**	jee	**Q**	kü	**X**	eeks
D	day	**K**	kah	**R**	airr	**Y**	ee-grek
E	er	**L**	el	**S**	ess	**Z**	zed
F	ef	**M**	em	**T**	tay		
G	jay	**N**	en	**U**	ü		

Here are two examples:

SMITH: ess em ee tay ahsh
JONES: jee oh en er ess

2

Checking In

Imagine yourself at the airport, speaking French to the clerk as you check in for a flight to Paris.

1. VOICI MON BILLET

Passenger: Bonjour, Madame. (Bong-joorr, Mah-dahm.)
Good morning.

Clerk: Bonjour, Monsieur . . . Madame. (Bong-joorr, Merss-yer . . . Mah-dahm.)
Good morning, Sir . . . Madam.

Passenger: Voici mon billet. Et voici le billet de ma femme. C'est le vol deux cent trois pour Paris. (Vwah-see mong bee-yay. Ay vwah-see ler bee-yay der mah fahm. Say ler vol der sahng trwah poorr Pah-ree.)
Here's my ticket. And here's my wife's ticket. It's flight two hundred and three for Paris.

Clerk: Merci. (Mairr-see.)
Thank you.

2. AVEZ-VOUS VOTRE PASSEPORT?

Clerk: Avez-vous votre passeport? (Ah-vay voo votr pahss-porr?)
Have you got your passport?

Passenger: Oui. Le voici. (Wee. Ler vwah-see.)
Yes. Here it is.

Clerk: Merci. Fumeurs ou non-fumeurs? (Mairr-see. Fü-merr oo nong fü-merr?)
Thank you. Smoking or non-smoking?

Passenger: Non-fumeurs, s'il vous plaît. (Nong-fü-merr, seel voo play.)
Non-smoking, please.

Clerk: Deux valises? (Der vah-leez?)
Two cases?
Passenger: Oui. Je garde le chat . . . pardon, le sac. (Wee. Jer gahrrd ler shah . . . pahrr-dong, ler sahk.)
Yes. I'm keeping the cat . . . sorry, the bag.
Clerk: Bien, Monsieur. (Byang, Merss-yer.)
Fine.

3. VÉRIFIEZ, MONSIEUR

Clerk: Voici les billets, les passeports et les cartes d'embarquement. C'est généralement la porte numéro neuf, mais vérifiez, Monsieur. (Vwah-see lay bee-yay, lay pahss-porr ay lay kahrrt dahng-bahrr-ker-mahng. Say jay-nay-rahl-mahng lah porrt nü-may-roh nerf, may vay-reef-yay, Merss-yer.)
Here are the tickets, the passports and the boarding passes. It's generally gate number nine, but check, Sir.
Passenger: Merci, Madame. (Mairr-see, Mah-dahm.)
Thank you.
Clerk: Bon voyage! (Bong vwah-yahj!)
Have a good trip!

INFORMATION

LA FRANCOPHONIE (FRENCH-SPEAKING COUNTRIES)

Once you have mastered this short course in French, you'll be surprised how far you'll be able to travel with your newly-acquired knowledge. France is, of course, our nearest neighbour and you can hop over (or under) the Channel and escape for a day or so in order to practise your French. But there are many other destinations in the world where French is spoken, although there might be some variations in the accent and in the use of certain words.

Let's begin a French world tour in Calais, then pass through France and enter the French-speaking part of Belgium, called "la Wallonie". Here you could take a leaf out of the locals' book and order **un plat de moules avec des frites** (mussels and chips). You may associate Belgium with the singer, Jacques Brel, who was very popular in France.

We can continue practising our French as we journey through **le grand-duché de Luxembourg**, the seat of the European Court of Justice, into Switzerland and the fascinating city of **Genève**.

Maybe you have more exotic tastes and prefer the fine weather of North Africa (**le Maroc, l'Algérie, la Tunisie**), called in French "**le Maghreb**", where, although Arabic is the first language, French is widely spoken as a result of the historical links with France.

If you are looking for something even more adventurous, you may choose to go deeper into Africa, to **le Tchad**, **le Sénégal, la Côte d'Ivoire**, and **le Zaïre**; or even further afield, to the Indian Ocean and the islands of **Madagascar** and **la Réunion.**

French, of course, is also spoken in Canada, in **Québec**, and you may remember the famous and controversial speech made there by General de Gaulle in 1967, which he ended with the words "**Vive le Québec libre!**"

La Martinique, la Guadeloupe, Haïti, Tahiti, le Viêt-nam . . . in these places too, *Just Enough French* will get you by!

LANGUAGE NOTES

BONJOUR!

"**Bonjour!**" means both "Good morning!" and "Good afternoon!"

"Good evening!" is "**Bonsoir!**" and when the French go to bed, they say "**Bonne nuit!**" (*Goodnight!*)

POLITE EXPRESSIONS

In polite conversation, it is usual to add "**Monsieur**" when speaking to a man and either "**Madame**" to a woman or "**Mademoiselle**" (mahd-mwah-zell) to a young woman.

You will quickly need "**merci**" (*thank you*) and "**s'il vous plaît**" (literally, *if it pleases you*) and also "**pardon**" (*excuse me*, or *I'm sorry*), so practise pronouncing these.

LE, LA AND LES

All French nouns are either masculine or feminine. To express "the" in French, we use "**le**" with the masculine and "**la**" with the feminine:

le billet (*the ticket*)   **la porte** (*the gate, the door*)
le passeport (*the passport*)   **la valise** (*the suitcase*)

Unfortunately, there's no way you can guess the gender of a noun, although sometimes, of course, it is obvious – for example, "**le monsieur**" (*gentleman*), "**la dame**" (*lady*). The best way to remember the gender of nouns is to learn them together with their "**le**" or "**la**". In the Word Lists at the end of each chapter in this book, the masculine and feminine nouns have been grouped, to help you.

In the plural, both "**le**" and "**la**" become "**les**":

les billets (*the tickets,* etc)   **les portes**
les passeports   **les valises**

MON, MA, MES

In the conversations you will also have noticed the words "**mon**" and "**ma**", for "my":

mon billet (*my ticket* – masculine noun)
ma femme (*my wife* – feminine noun)
mes billets (*my tickets* – masculine plural)
mes valises (*my suitcases* – feminine plural)

VOTRE, VOS

The word for "your" is "**votre**" (with all singular nouns) and "**vos**" with all plural nouns:

votre billet   **vos billets**
votre femme   **vos valises**

VOICI

This useful word means "Here is" and "Here are".

"Here it is" is **"Le voici"** (if the "it" refers to a masculine noun) and **"La voici"** (if the "it" refers to a feminine noun). **"Les voici"** means "Here they are".

Voici mon billet.	**Le voici.**
Voici ma valise.	**La voici.**
Voici mes valises.	**Les voici.**

GÉNÉRALEMENT

The ending **"ment"** in French often corresponds to "ly" in English, as in **"généralement"** (*generally*). Here are some others, whose meaning you will have no trouble in guessing:

rapidement   probablement   certainement   immédiatement

 NUMBERS

It is important to be able to handle numbers, so straightaway learn to count from one to ten, and the word for 100:

1	**un** (erng)	6	**six** (seess)
2	**deux** (der)	7	**sept** (set)
3	**trois** (trwah)	8	**huit** (ü'eet, or less accurately, weet)
4	**quatre** (kahtr)	9	**neuf** (nerf)
5	**cinq** (sangk)	10	**dix** (deess)
100	**cent** (sahng)		

YOUR TURN

 1. WHAT WOULD YOU SAY IN FRENCH WHEN:

a. You show your boarding pass to the stewardess on the plane. (Begin **"Voici . . . "**)

b. You want to ask for seats in the smoking section.

c. You want to thank the steward for showing you your seat.

d. You are travelling with four suitcases, and the check-in clerk asks: **"Deux valises?"**

e.You greet the female receptionist at your hotel at 2.00 pm.

f.You have been told that you don't in fact have a booking and you want the receptionist to check.

g.You want to tell the check-in clerk that you will keep the small bag with you. (You may need to look up the word for "small" in the Mini-Dictionary at the back of the book.)

h.You are unpacking and you say to yourself "Ah, here's my umbrella."

i.You are checking with your companion that he or she has everything for the journey:

i) Have you got your suitcase?

ii) Have you got your passport?

iii) Have you got your cat?

You can check your answers with the key on page 101.

2. WHAT PRICE?

Listen to the tape and fill in the prices of the items shown below.
You can check your answers with the key on page 101.

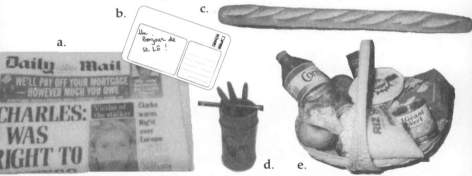

FORGET-ME-NOT

You will have noticed how similar some French and English words and expressions are: for instance, "**le passeport**", "**généralement**", "**avez-vous**". On the other hand, there may not seem to be any similarity – for instance, between "**le vol**" and "*flight*". And yet, if you think a little more about it, there is a link. We might call someone who "flies off the handle" "volatile". Again, the French word for "*to smoke*" is "**fumer**" – it seems quite different until you think of the English word "to fume" – "to give off smoke". Finding such links between French and English words is a good way of remembering new words as you come across them. In each chapter you will find a "FORGET-ME-NOT" section suggesting some word associations to start you off – but we hope you will find this method of memorising words useful and so go on to look for other associations for yourselves.

French word	English association
la porte (*gate, door*)	portal (gateway)
garder (*to keep*)	to guard (keep safe)
sept (*seven*)	septet
cent (*hundred*)	per cent

WORD LIST

MASCULINE NOUNS

le billet	ticket
le chat	cat
le monsieur	gentleman
le numéro	number
le passeport	passport
le sac	bag
le vol	flight
le voyage	journey

FEMININE NOUNS

la carte	card
la carte d'embarquement	boarding pass
la dame	lady
la femme	wife, woman
la porte	door, gate
la valise	suitcase

Avez-vous . . . ?	Do you have . . . ?, Have you got . . . ?
Bien	Fine, Good
Bonjour!	Good morning!, Good afternoon!
Bonne nuit!	Goodnight!
Bonsoir!	Good evening!
Bon voyage!	Have a good journey!
certainement	certainly
C'est . . .	It is . . .
et	and
fumeurs ou non-fumeurs	smoking or non-smoking (literally, smokers or non-smokers)
généralement	generally

immédiatement	immediately
je garde	I keep, I'm keeping, I'll keep
mais	but
merci	thank you
non	no
ou	or
oui	yes
pour	for
probablement	probably
rapidement	quickly
s'il vous plaît	please
Vérifiez!	Check!
voici . . .	here is . . .

3 Destination Paris

Try speaking French on the plane to Paris.

1. C'EST À GAUCHE

Steward: Bonjour, Madame. Bonjour, Monsieur. Quels numéros avez-vous? (Bong-joorr, Mah-dahm. Bong-joorr, Merss-yer. Kell nü-may-roh ah-vay voo?)
Good morning, Madam. Good morning, Sir. What seat numbers do you have?

Passenger: Euh . . . nous avons les places neuf et dix. (Er . . . noo zah-vong lay plahss nerf ay deess.)
Er . . . we have got seat numbers nine and ten.

Steward: C'est à gauche, Madame – Non! Excusez-moi! C'est à droite. (Say tah gohsh, Mah-dahm – Nong! Eks-kü-zay-mwah! Say tah drwaht.)
That's on the left, Madam – No! I'm sorry! It's on the right.

2. VOULEZ-VOUS ATTACHER VOTRE CEINTURE?

Steward: Madame, voulez-vous attacher votre ceinture, s'il vous plaît? (Mah-dahm, voo-lay voo ah-tah-shay votr sang-tür, seel voo play?)
Madam, would you fasten your seat-belt, please?

Passenger: Oh, excusez-moi! . . . Où est la ceinture? (Oh, eks-kü-zay-mwah! . . . Oo ay lah sang-tür?)
Oh, I'm sorry! . . . Where is the belt?

Steward: La voici. Monsieur, voulez-vous mettre le sac sous votre siège? . . . Merci. (Lah vwah-see. Merss-yer, voo-lay voo metr ler sahk soo votr syej? . . . Mairr-see.)
Here it is. Sir, would you put the bag under your seat? . . . Thank you.

3. DU CAFÉ?

Steward: Du café, Madame? Du thé, du jus d'orange? (Dü kah-fay, Mah-dahm? Dü tay, dü jü do-rahngj?)
Some coffee, Madam? Some tea, some orange juice?

Passenger: Un café et un jus d'orange, s'il vous plaît. Et . . . pourriez-vous m'apporter du lait . . . dans une soucoupe? (Erng kah-fay ay erng jü do-rahngj, seel voo play. Ay . . . poo-ryay voo mah-porr-tay dü lay . . . dahng zün soo-koop?)
A coffee and an orange juice, please. And . . . please could you bring me some milk . . . in a saucer?

Steward: Oui, Madame . . . Ah, ces Anglais! (Wee, Mah-dahm . . . Ah, say zAhng-glay!)
Yes, Madam . . . Oh, these English!

4. DÉSIREZ-VOUS ACHETER QUELQUE CHOSE?

Steward: Désirez-vous acheter quelque chose, Madame? (Day-zee-ray voo ahsh-tay kell-ker shohz, Mah-dahm?)
Do you wish to buy something, Madam?

Passenger: Oui. Deux cents cigarettes . . . et du parfum, s'il vous plaît. (Wee. Der sahng see-gah-ret . . . ay dü pahr-ferng, seel voo play.)
Yes. Two hundred cigarettes . . . and some perfume, please.

Steward: Oui. Quel parfum? (Wee. Kell pahr-ferng?)
Yes. Which perfume?

Passenger: Chanel numéro cinq. (Shah-nell nü-may-roh sangk.)
Chanel number five.

INFORMATION

WHICH WAY TO FRANCE?

By air

You are, of course, already aware of the many flights to the Continent offered by the large airlines, but you may be less familiar with the smaller companies such as Brit Air and Air

Vendée, which serve Normandy and Brittany and operate from London, Gatwick. ATS Vulcan will fly you from Southampton to Cherbourg and Caen.

By sea

If you're taking your car (or bicycle), then you will need to choose one of the ferry companies – and so enjoy a mini-cruise on a luxurious, modern ship, with tempting shops, excellent restaurants and bars, comfortable lounges, and floor shows, a cinema and a casino to entertain you. The moment you go on board, you will smell the distinctive aroma of French coffee and **tarte aux pommes** (apple tart) coming from the **salon de thé**. The hovercraft (**l'aéroglisseur**) and the Seacat are a boon for travellers in a hurry to cross the Channel.

By land

It may be that you are not a good sailor (**vous n'avez pas le pied marin**), in which case you should take **le Shuttle** and go through the Channel Tunnel. There are frequent departures from Folkestone and the crossing to Calais takes 35 minutes. No booking is necessary; just turn up and buy a ticket. The actual journey times are:

London – Paris	3 hours
London – Lille	2 hours
London – Brussels	3 hours 10 minutes

Whichever way you choose to get across the Channel (**La Manche**), we wish you **Bon voyage!**

LANGUAGE NOTES

WHAT . . . ?/WHICH . . . ?

The steward asked "**Quels numéros avez-vous?**" (*What numbers do you have?*)

The word "**quel**" changes depending on whether it comes in front of a masculine, feminine, singular or plural noun:

Quel vol? (m.) (*Which flight?*)
Quelle place? (f.) (*Which seat?*)
Quels billets? (m.pl.) (*Which tickets?*)
Quelles valises? (f.pl.) (*Which suitcases?*)

ASKING QUESTIONS

Some questions begin with a question word, like "**Quel . . . ?**"
Others don't:

Quelles places avez-vous? (*Which seats do you have?*)
Avez-vous la valise? (*Do you have/Have you got the suitcase?*)

In both cases, the position of the subject and verb is reversed
from the normal:

Vous avez la valise. (*You have the suitcase.*)
Avez-vous la valise? (*Do you have the suitcase?*)

Mind you, very often in conversation the French turn a
statement into a question simply by using a rising intonation:

Vous avez la valise?
Vous parlez anglais?

WOULD YOU MIND . . . ?

To ask someone politely to do something, you can use
"**Voulez-vous**" or "**Pourriez-vous**":

Voulez-vous attacher votre ceinture? (*Would you fasten your
seatbelt?*)
Voulez-vous mettre le sac sous votre siège? (*Would you put
the bag under your seat?*)
Voulez-vous remplir cette fiche? (*Would you fill in this card?*)
Pourriez-vous m'apporter un verre d'eau? (*Please would you
bring me a glass of water?*)
Pourriez-vous m'apporter un journal anglais/français?
(*Please would you bring me an English/French newspaper?*)

"**Voulez-vous**" and "**Pourriez-vous**" are followed by the
infinitive (dictionary form) – "**attacher**" (*to fasten*), "**remplir**"
(*to fill in*), "**apporter**" (*to bring*). The "**er**", "**ir**" and "**re**" on the
end of the French words corresponds to the English "to".

AVOIR – TO HAVE

"To have" and "to be" are two key verbs to know. They have their own irregular forms.

j'ai (*I have*)   **nous avons** (*we have*)
vous avez (*you have*)*
il a (*he/it has*)   **ils ont** (*they have*)
elle a (*she/it has*)   **elles ont** (*they have* – if "they" are all
                                      feminine)

Here is the imitated pronunciation:

jay, voo zah-vay, eel ah, ell ah, noo zah-vong, eel zong, ell zong.

Notice how the "**s**" of "**nous**", "**vous**", "**ils**" and "**elles**" is carried over to the next word and pronounced like a "z". This happens a great deal in French and is called "liaison".

ÊTRE – TO BE

je suis (*I am*)   **nous sommes** (*we are*)
vous êtes (*you are*)*
il est (*he/it is*)   **ils sont** (*they are*)
elle est (*she/it is*)   **elles sont** (they are – if "they" are all
                                      feminine)

Notice the liaison in these examples.

il est marié (eel ay mahrr-yay) *he's married*
elle est divorcée (ell ay dee-vorr-say) *she's divorced*
nous sommes célibataires (noo som say-lee-bah-tairr) *we're single*
vous êtes en vacances (voo zet ahng vah-kahng-ss) *you're on holiday*
ils sont ingénieurs (eel song tang-jayn-yerr) *they're* (masculine) *engineers*
elles sont ici pour affaires (ell song tee-see poorr ah-fairr) *they're* (feminine) *here on business*

*   Note: As well as "**vous**" for "you", French has a familiar form, "**tu**" – which is used among friends and to children. In order not to complicate this course for you, we are giving only the "**vous**" and not the "**tu**" forms of verbs. You will never be wrong in using "**vous**" with the French people you speak to.

OÙ EST . . . ?

Learn well the expressions "**Où est . . . ?**" (*Where is . . . ?*) and "**Où sont . . . ?**" (*Where are . . . ?*), for you will need them all the time. Among the answers you might get are:

C'est à gauche. (Say tah gohsh.) *It's on the left.*
C'est à droite. (Say tah drwaht.) *It's on the right.*
C'est tout droit. (Say too drwah.) *It's straight on.*
Ils sont sur la table. (Eel song sür lah tahbl.) *They are on the table.*
Ils sont sous la table. (Eel song soo lah tahbl.) *They are under the table.*

Notice how liaison happens again with "**C'est à**".

UN, UNE

These are the masculine and feminine forms for "a":

un café (*a coffee*)
un jus d'orange (*an orange juice*)
une salade (*a salad*)
une glace (*an ice cream*)

DU, DE LA, DES

These words mean "some" in front of masculine, feminine and plural nouns:

du café (*some coffee*)
du jus d'orange (*some orange juice*)
de la salade (*some salad*)
de la glace (*some ice cream*)
de la crème (*some cream*)
des cigarettes (*some cigarettes*)

AH, CES ANGLAIS! – AND OTHER NATIONALITIES

To say you are English, if you are male, you say "**Je suis Anglais**" (Ahng-glay). If you are female, you say "**Je suis Anglaise**" (Ahng-glez).

Here are some other nationalities, in their masculine and feminine forms:

Scottish	**Écossais** (Ay-ko-say)	**Écossaise** (Ay-ko-sez)
Welsh	**Gallois** (Gahl-wah)	**Galloise** (Gahl-wahz)
Irish	**Irlandais** (Eer-lahng-day)	**Irlandaise** (Eer-lahng-dez)
American	**Américain** (Ah-may-ree-kang)	**Américaine** (Ah-may-ree-kenn)
Canadian	**Canadien** (Kah-nah-dyang)	**Canadienne** (Kah-nah-dyenn)
Australian	**Australien** (Oh-strah-lyang)	**Australienne** (Oh-strah-lyenn)

CE, CETTE, CES

These are the masculine, feminine and plural forms for "this" and "these".

ce parapluie (m.) (*this umbrella*)
cette ceinture (f.) (*this belt*)
ces vols (m. pl.) (*these flights*)
ces oranges (f. pl.) (*these oranges*)

YOUR TURN

1. COULD YOU COPE?

a. In the hustle and bustle at the airport, you accidentally hit a lady with your "**parapluie**". What do you say?

b. At the hotel the receptionist says: "**Voulez-vous signer cette fiche, s'il vous plaît?**" What does this mean?

c. You come down to breakfast next morning, but don't know where to sit. How would you ask "Which table, please?"

d. The French breakfast normally consists of rolls, croissants or French bread (**baguette**), but the waiter or waitress will always need to know what you prefer to drink. Ask for orange juice and coffee with milk.

e. The milk has been forgotten. Say "Could you bring me some milk, please?"

f. You're looking for the underground and you ask a passer-by "**Où est le métro, s'il vous plaît?**" You receive the reply "**C'est tout droit.**" What does this mean?

g. You're actually Scottish, but for some reason the waiter thinks you're American. Put him straight (you're female).

h. This time you're in London and a French tourist stops you and says "**Pardon, Monsieur, vous parlez français? Où est la pharmacie, s'il vous plaît?**" Look at the plan below and give directions.

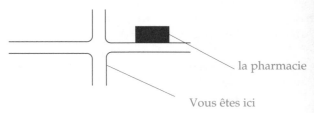

la pharmacie

Vous êtes ici

2. ON THE PLANE

Take part in this dialogue, using the tape if you can. You can check your answers with the key on page 101.

You: Where's seat number 7, please?
Stewardess: **À gauche, Monsieur.**
You: Thank you.
(You discover that a French lady has taken your seat by mistake.) Excuse me. This is my seat. Here's my boarding pass – seat number 7.(The passenger smiles, apologises and moves to another part of the plane.)
Stewardess: **Désirez-vous un journal français, Monsieur?**
You: No thank you. Could you bring me a glass of water? (She brings the water, but almost trips over your umbrella.)
Stewardess: **Voulez-vous mettre le parapluie sous votre siège, s'il vous plaît?**
You: I'm sorry, but it's too large!

FORGET-ME-NOT

French word	English association
à droite (*on the right*)	adroit (doing things right)
la fiche (*card*)	microfiche
le lait (*milk*)	chocolate
parler (*to speak*)	parliament
sur (*on*)	surface

24

WORD LIST

MASCULINE NOUNS

l'aéroglisseur*	hovercraft
le café	coffee
l'ingénieur	engineer
le journal	newspaper
le jus d'orange	orange juice
le lait	milk
le métro	underground
le parapluie	umbrella
le pied	foot
le salon	lounge
le siège	seat
le thé	tea
le verre	glass

* Both "le" and "la" become "l'" when the noun begins with a vowel.

acheter	to buy
apporter	to bring
attacher	to fasten
avoir	to have
désirer	to want
être	to be
louer	to hire
mettre	to put
parler	to speak
payer	to pay
remplir	to fill (in)
réserver	to reserve

FEMININE NOUNS

les affaires	business
la ceinture	belt
la cigarette	cigarette
la crème	cream
l'eau*	water
la fiche	card
la glace	ice cream
la Manche	the Channel
l'orange*	orange
la pharmacie	chemist's
la place	seat
la pomme	apple
la salade	salad
la soucoupe	saucer
la table	table
la tarte	tart
les vacances	holidays

à droite	on the right
à gauche	on the left
célibataire	single
dans	in
divorcé	divorced
marié	married
où?	where?
sous	under
sur	on
tout droit	straight on

4 At the Hotel

Imagine your plane has landed and the few formalities at Charles de Gaulle airport are over. You've taken the coach to Étoile and found a charming, small hotel just off the Champs-Elysées.

1. JE VOUDRAIS UNE CHAMBRE

Guest: Bonsoir, Madame. Je voudrais une chambre pour deux personnes avec salle de bains, s'il vous plaît. (Bong-swahrr, Mah-dahm. Jer voo-dray ün shahng-br poorr der pairr-sonn ah-vek sahl der bang, seel voo play.)
Good evening. I would like a double room with bathroom, please.

Reception: Un instant, Monsieur . . . Je regrette, mais nous avons seulement une grande chambre pour trois

personnes avec douche. (Erng nang-
stahng, Merss-yer . . . Jer rer-gret, may noo zah-
vong serl-mahng ün grahng-d shahng-br poor
trwah pair-sonn ah-vek doosh.)
One moment, Sir . . . I'm sorry, but we have only a large
room for three, with shower.

Guest: Quel est le prix de la chambre? (Kell ay ler pree der
lah shahng-br?)
What is the price of the room?

Reception: Cinq cents francs par nuit. Le petit déjeuner est en
supplément – trente francs. (Sang-(k) sahng frahng
pahrr nü'ee. Ler ptee day-jer-nay ay tahng sü-play-
mahng – trahng-t frahng.)
Five hundred francs per night. Breakfast is extra –
thirty francs.

2. LES CHATS NE SONT PAS ADMIS!

Guest: J'ai un . . . un petit chat dans mon sac. Vous
acceptez les chats? (Jay erng . . . erng p'tee shah
dahng mong sahk. Voo zahk-sep-tay lay shah?)
I have a . . . a little cat in my bag. Do you accept cats?

Reception: Ah non, Monsieur! Les chiens et les chats ne sont
pas admis dans l'hôtel! (Ah nong, Merss-yer! Lay
shyang ay lay shah ner song pah ahd-mee dahng
loh-tell!)
Oh no, Sir! Dogs and cats are not allowed in the hotel!

Guest: C'est une chambre pour trois personnes? (Say tün
shahng-br poorr trwah pairr-sonn?)
It's a room for three people?

Reception: Oui. (Wee.)
Yes.

Guest: Eh bien, nous allons la prendre, mais dans ce cas-là
vous acceptez notre chat. (Ay byang, noo zah-long
lah prahng-dr, may dahng ser kah lah voo zahk-
sep-tay notr shah.)
Well, we're going to take it, but in that case, you can
accept our cat.

Reception: Euh . . . d'accord . . . exceptionnellement. (Er . . .
dah-korr . . . ek-sep-syo-nell-mahng.)
Er . . . OK . . . as an exception.

3. VOUS MANGEZ À L'HÔTEL?

Reception: Vous mangez à l'hôtel ce soir? (Voo mahng-jay ah loh-tell ser swahrr?)
You'll be eating at the hotel this evening?

Guest: Oui, c'est ça. (Wee, say sah.)
Yes, that's right.

Reception: Est-ce que je réserve une table pour deux . . . ou pour trois, Monsieur? (Ess-ker jer ray-zairrv ün tahbl poorr der . . . oo poorr trwah, Merss-yer?)
Do I reserve a table for two . . . or for three, Sir?

INFORMATION

FRENCH HOTELS

French hotels are classified according to their comfort and the facilities they offer. This comfort ranges from one star (**une étoile**), plain but fairly comfortable, to five stars (**cinq étoiles**), very luxurious. Prices vary according to the number of stars and the particular region. Paris hotels, of course, are more expensive than those in Brittany, for example.

The price
The price of a room is normally displayed both outside the hotel and inside the room itself. The important thing to remember is that the price quoted is for the room, not per person. Breakfast is charged extra.

Credit cards
All the usual credit cards are normally accepted, but note that Access is referred to as "Mastercard".

Business groups
The larger hotel chains (Novotel, Mercure, Sofitel, etc) also cater for business groups and offer special rates.

Logis de France
These are family-run hotels and are usually found outside built-up areas. The prices are very reasonable and you can always be sure of a warm welcome. There's often a restaurant offering local dishes.

OTHER FORMS OF ACCOMMODATION

Chambres d'hôte

These are the equivalent of the British bed and breakfast. You'll often find them in villages, in the countryside and in renovated farmhouses. The price will include both room and breakfast, unlike at the hotels. When driving in France, you'll see a sign by the side of the road which reads, for example:

> **Chambre d'hôte**
>
> **1ère à droite**

Gîtes de France

These are self-catering holiday homes. See Chapter 9.

Bonnes vacances!

LANGUAGE NOTES

JE VOUDRAIS

"**Je voudrais**" (*I would like*) must be one of the most useful expressions you can learn – it will get you what you want!

C'EST ÇA

Another useful expression is: "**C'est ça**" (*That's right*).

MORE NUMBERS

11	**onze** (ongz)	14	**quatorze** (kah-torrz)
12	**douze** (dooz)	15	**quinze** (kangz)
13	**treize** (trez)	30	**trente** (trahng-t)

SOME EXPRESSIONS OF TIME

aujourd'hui (*today*)	**cette semaine** (*this week*)
ce soir (*this evening*)	**demain** (*tomorrow*)
cet après-midi (*this afternoon*)	**hier** (*yesterday*)

UNE PERSONNE

Surprisingly, the word for "person" (**la personne**) is always feminine, even if it refers to a man.

UNE GRANDE CHAMBRE

If you look up in a French dictionary the word for "large", you will find **"grand"** – so why is "a large room" **"une grande chambre"**? Adjectives, such as **"grand"**, **"petit"** (*small*), **"intelligent"**, change their form depending on whether they are describing masculine, feminine or plural nouns. E.g.:

un petit sac (m.)   **une petite valise** (f.)
les petits sacs   **les petites valises**
le monsieur est intelligent **la dame est intelligente**

QUEL EST LE PRIX DE . . . ?

We saw on page 19 how **"quel"** changes its form in front of a noun. It also changes in expressions like the following:

Quel est le prix de . . . ? (*What is the price of . . . ?*)
Quel est votre nom? (*What is your name?*)
Quelle est votre adresse? (*What's your address?*)

NE . . . PAS

The English "not" is expressed in French by two words, **"ne"** and **"pas"**. **"Ne"** goes in front of the verb and **"pas"** after it.

je garde (*I keep*)   **je ne garde pas** (*I do not keep*)
je suis (*I am*)   **je ne suis pas** (*I am not*)
vous vérifiez (*you check*)   **vous ne vérifiez pas** (*you do not check*)
les chiens sont admis   **les chiens ne sont pas admis**
  (*dogs are allowed*)   (*dogs are not allowed*)

VERB ENDINGS

You have learnt the verbs **"avoir"** (*to have*) and **"être"** (*to be*) (page 21), with their irregular forms. Other verbs follow a more regular pattern. Verbs ending in **"er"**, such as **"garder"** (*to keep*) and **"téléphoner"**, go like this in the present tense:

je garde (*I keep*)   **nous gardons** (*we keep*)
vous gardez (*you keep*)
il garde (*he/it keeps*)   **ils gardent** (*they* – masculine – *keep*)
elle garde (*she/it keeps*)   **elles gardent** (*they* – feminine – *keep*)

je téléphone (*I telephone*)   **nous téléphonons** (*we telephone*)
vous téléphonez (*you telephone*)
il/elle téléphone   **ils/elles téléphonent**
  (*he/she telephones*)   (*they telephone*)

EST-CE QUE . . . ?

You already know two ways of asking questions in French:

Parlez-vous anglais?
Vous parlez anglais? (with rising intonation)

A third way of asking this question is:

Est-ce que vous parlez anglais?

YOUR TURN

1. COULD YOU COPE?

a. Tell the French hotel receptionist that you would like a single room.

b. You've forgotten to add "with bathroom, please".

c. The receptionist has mentioned the price of the room, 350F, but you're not sure if breakfast is extra. Find out.

d. You find a few problems in your room. Go back to reception and say:
  i) The radio doesn't work
  ii) The toilet doesn't work
  iii) The lift is out of order
  iv) The bed is too small

e. The receptionist asks "**Est-ce que vous mangez à l'hôtel ce soir?**" Reply that you are not, but perhaps tomorrow.

f. Next morning at breakfast the young waitress has served cold coffee. Call her and tell her.

g. When the time comes to settle the bill, ask "Do you accept credit cards?"

h. Later you decide to have lunch in a very popular restaurant. It's a good idea to book in advance. Telephone and say "Good morning. I'd like to reserve a table for two – for midday."

i. On the way to the restaurant you pass a hotel that has these signs outside. What do they mean, in French?

VISA MASTERCARD AMERICAN EXPRESS	HôTEL * * *	We speak English	

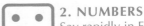 **2. NUMBERS**
Say rapidly in French: 12 9 15 4 11 13 14 7 2 5.
Check your answers with the tape, if you can.

FORGET-ME-NOT

French word	English association
la chambre (*bedroom*)	chamber
la douche (*shower*)	to douse
hier (*yesterday*)	the word sounds a little like the first syllable of "yesterday"
manger (*to eat*)	manger
le matin (*morning*)	matins
seulement (*only*)	solely

WORD LIST

MASCULINE NOUNS

l'après-midi	afternoon*
le cas	case
le chien	dog
le déjeuner	lunch
le franc	franc
l'hôtel†	hotel
l'instant	instant, moment
le matin	morning
le petit déjeuner	breakfast
le prix	price
le soir	evening
le supplément	supplement

FEMININE NOUNS

la chambre	(bed)room
la douche	shower
l'étoile	star
la nuit	night
la personne	person
la salle	room
la salle de bain(s)	bathroom
la semaine	week

* "**l'apres-midi**" can, in fact, be either masculine or feminine
† "**le**" and "**la**" become "**l'**" in front of most words beginning with "h", as well as in front of words beginning with vowels.

accepter	toaccept
manger	to eat
prendre	to take
regretter	to be sorry
téléphoner (à)	to telephone
admis	allowed
aujourd'hui	today
avec	with
dans ce cas-là	in that case
demain	tomorrow
en supplément	extra
exceptionnellement	exceptionally
grand	big, large
hier	yesterday
intelligent	intelligent
petit	small
pour	for
seulement	only
Je vais (manger)	I'm going (to eat)
Nous allons (réserver)	We're going (to reserve)
Je voudrais	I would like
Un instant, s'il vous plaît	One moment, please

5 In the Restaurant

Imagine it is 8 o'clock in the evening, you're hungry and looking forward to your evening meal in the hotel restaurant.

1. NOUS AVONS RÉSERVÉ UNE TABLE

Waitress: Bonsoir Madame. Bonsoir Monsieur.
Good evening, Madam. Good evening, Sir.

Guest: Bonsoir. Nous avons réservé une table. Pour huit heures.
Good evening. We've reserved a table. For eight o'clock.

Waitress: Oui, Monsieur. C'est à quel nom?
Yes, Sir. What name is it?

Guest: Martin.

Waitress: Oui, Monsieur. Par ici, s'il vous plaît.
Yes, Sir. This way, please.

2. LE MENU OU LA CARTE?

Waitress: Voilà, Monsieur. C'est une bonne table près de la fenêtre.
Here you are, Sir. It's a good table, near the window.

Guest: Merci beaucoup.
Thank you very much.

Waitress: Vous prenez le menu ou la carte?
Are you taking the set menu or eating à la carte?

Guest: Le menu.
The set menu.

3. VOUS AVEZ CHOISI?

Waitress: Vous avez choisi?
Have you chosen?

Guest: Oui. Pour commencer . . . un saumon fumé . . . et une terrine pour moi.
Yes. To begin with . . . one smoked salmon . . . and a pâté for me.

Waitress: Bien, Monsieur. Et ensuite?
Fine, Sir. And then?

MENU 120F
Crudités variées
Saumon fumé *Terrine du chef*
Truite aux amandes *Canard à l'orange* *Tournedos grillé*
Légumes de saison *Plateau de fromages*
Pâtisseries ou Glaces

Guest: Une truite aux amandes et un canard à l'orange.
One trout with almonds and one duck in orange sauce.

Waitress: Et comme boisson?
And to drink?

Guest: Une bouteille de Muscadet.
A bottle of Muscadet.

Waitress: Oui, Monsieur. Vous prenez un apéritif?
Yes, Sir. Are you having an aperitif?

Guest: Oui. Un porto et un whisky.
Yes. A port and a whisky.

Waitress: Très bien, Monsieur.
Very good, Sir.

Guest: Merci.
Thank you.

4. ET COMME DESSERT?

Waitress: Et comme dessert, Monsieur?
And for dessert, Sir?

Guest: Deux glaces au café.
Two coffee ice creams.

35

INFORMATION

A GASTRONOMIC TOUR

There are many aspects of France that attract the foreign tourist, not least, of course, its reputation for good food and good wines. Come on a gastronomic tour of some regions of France:

Normandy

Most recipes in Normandy include cream and/or Calvados (apple brandy). A well-known traditional dish is **la poule au blanc**, which consists of boiled fowl and vegetables, served with hot, thick cream. You might like to be more adventurous and try a very famous dish associated with this region, namely **les tripes à la mode de Caen**. This is prepared with tripe, vegetables, cider and Calvados and has to be cooked for at least eight hours!

Brittany

Brittany is renowned for its seafood and its pancakes. Make sure you try **le homard** (lobster) and **les langoustines** (type of very large prawn) and do go along to a **crêperie** and enjoy some of the many varieties of pancakes on offer.

The Southwest

If you're visiting this region, you must sample **le cassoulet**, a stew made with haricot beans, pork, goose or duck, sausages, garlic and herbs.

Provence

In addition to the wonderful sunny weather, we feel sure you'll like **la bouillabaisse**, a thick Mediterranean fish soup, served with garlic mayonnaise called **la rouille**, "rust" (because of its colour), and **croûtons**. This dish is a complete meal in itself.

Alsace

If you're staying in Alsace, you're bound to be offered the speciality of the region – **la choucroute**, a dish made with special, locally grown cabbage, pork, sausages, onions, juniper berries and white wine.

SOME QUALITY WINES

Bordeaux wines
These, of course, can be red or white. Some examples of
excellent, but perhaps expensive red wines are: **Château
Margaux, St-Emilion, Pomerol.** And some white wines:
Sauternes, Entre-Deux-Mers.

Burgundy wines
Red: **Nuits-St-Georges, Clos Vougeot, Pommard.**
White: **Chablis, Pouilly-Fuissé.**

Alsace wines
These are normally white, dry wines such as **Sylvaner,
Riesling, Gewurztraminer.**

There are also many good and inexpensive local wines such as
those of the Loire, Côtes du Rhône and Provence.

Bon appétit! À votre bonne santé!

LANGUAGE NOTES

VOILÀ

You will find this a useful word, rather like "**Voici**"(page 14).
"**Voilà**" means "There's . . . " or "Here's . . . " or simply "Here
you are" (as when the waiter or waitress hands you your
soup).

COMME

"**Comme**" normally means "like" as in "**comme ça**" (*like that*).
But it can also mean "in the way of", as when the waiter or
waitress asks: "**Et comme boisson?**" (*And to drink?*)

MORE NUMBERS

16	**seize** (sez)	19	**dix-neuf** (deez-nerf)
17	**dix-sept** (dee-set)	20	**vingt** (vang)
18	**dix-huit** (dee-zü'eet)		

37

TELLING THE TIME

It's important to get the time right; otherwise you might miss the coach or an important meeting. You might ask:

Quelle heure est-il? (*What time is it?*)

The reply might be:

Il est une heure. (*It's one o'clock.*)
Il est deux heures. (*It's two o'clock.*)
Il est trois heures et quart. (*It's quarter past three.*)
Il est trois heures vingt. (*It's three twenty.*)
Il est quatre heures et demie. (*It's half past four.*)
Il est dix heures moins le quart. (*It's quarter to ten.*)
Il est onze heures moins dix. (*It's ten to eleven.*)
Il est midi. (*It's midday.*)
Il est minuit. (*It's midnight.*)

Or you might ask "**A quelle heure . . . ?**"
(*At what time/When . . . ?*) and the answer could be:

À une heure (*At one o'clock*)
À trois heures et demie (*At half past three*)
À minuit (*At midnight*)

THE PAST TENSE

In the conversations in the restaurant, we see how the French talk about the past, using the verb "**avoir**" (see page 21):

Nous avons réservé une table. (*We reserved a table.*)
Vous avez choisi? (*Have you chosen?*)

Here are some more examples of the past tense of verbs ending in "**er**":

J'ai réservé. (*I have reserved./I reserved.*)
Il a parlé. (*He has spoken./He spoke.*)
Elle a gardé . . . (*She has kept . . . /She kept . . .*)
Nous avons loué . . . (*We have hired . . . /We hired . . .*)
Vous avez téléphoné. (*You have telephoned./You telephoned.*)
Ils ont mangé. (*They have eaten./They ate.*)
Elles ont vérifié. (*They have checked./They checked.*)

Verbs ending in "er" form the past with "é". Verbs ending in "ir" form the past with "i" (as in "**Vous avez choisi?**").

THE VERB "PRENDRE"

The verb "**prendre**" (*to take*) goes like this in the present tense:

je prends (*I take*)   **nous prenons** (*we take*)
vous prenez (*you take*)
il/elle prend (*he/she takes*)   **ils/elles prennent** (*they take*)

In the past, it goes like this:

j'ai pris (*I took/have taken*)   **nous avons pris** (*we took/have taken*)
vous avez pris (*you took/have taken*)
il/elle a pris   **ils/elles ont pris**
  (*he/she took/has taken*)   (*they took/have taken*)

POSITION WORDS

You already know "**sur**" and "**sous**" and will have noticed "**près de la fenêtre**" (*near the window*) in conversation 2. Here are some more position words:

à côté de (*next to, by*)   **en face de** (*opposite*)
derrière (*behind*)   **loin de** (*far from*)
devant (*in front of*)

DU, DE LA, DES

"**De**" plus "**le**" contract to "**du**":

L'hôtel est près du restaurant. (*The hotel is near the restaurant.*)

"**De**" plus "**la**" remain as "**de la**":

L'hôtel est en face de la gare. (*The hotel is opposite the station.*)

"**De**" plus "**l**" plus apostrophe remain as "**de l'**":

Le restaurant est loin de l'hôtel. (*The restaurant is far away from the hotel.*)

"**De**" plus "**les**" contract to "**des**":

Le cinéma est en face des magasins. (*The cinema is opposite the shops.*)

AU, À LA, AUX

The little word "**à**" means "at" or "to". Like "**de**", when it is followed by "**le**", the two words contract to "**au**", and when it is followed by "**les**", the two words contract to "**aux**":

Je vais au cinéma. (*I'm going to the cinema.*)
Je vais à la gare. (*I'm going to the station.*)
Je vais à l'hôtel. (*I'm going to the hotel.*)
Je vais aux États-Unis. (*I'm going to the United States.*)

FOR ME AND YOU

After a word like "**pour**" (*for*), you need the following forms:

pour moi (*for me*)   **pour nous** (*for us*)
pour vous (*for you*)
pour lui (*for him*)   **pour eux** (*for them*, masc.)
pour elle (*for her*)   **pour elles** (*for them*, fem.)

FALSE FRIENDS

You could be forgiven for thinking that "**une glace au café**" meant "a glass of coffee", because that's what it sounds like. But "**une glace**", in fact, is an ice cream.

Here are some more words, which don't mean what they might immediately appear to. Learn them carefully!

le car (*coach*)   **charger** (*to load*)
la librairie (*bookshop*)   **demander** (*to ask for*)
le pétrole (*petroleum*)

YOUR TURN

1. COULD YOU COPE?

a. Imagine that you're telling a French acquaintance what you did during the first week of your stay in France. Say:
We reserved a room in a small hotel.
We spoke French.
We hired a car.
We ate in a good restaurant.
We phoned (to) our daughter in England.

b. You have just arrived at a French restaurant. How would you say "Good evening! We've reserved a table for two, for half past eight."?

c. The waiter replies "**Ah oui. Vous êtes les clients anglais qui ont téléphoné ce matin.**" What does this mean?

d. He continues: "**Voulez-vous passer par ici, s'il vous plaît?**" What does this mean?

e. He takes you to your table which, frankly, could be better situated. Say to him: "Could we have a table near the window, please?"

f. After you have sat down and had a chance to look at the various menus, say: "We've chosen the set menu at 120F."

g. During the booking of an excursion to Versailles, you're told that the coach leaves at "**huit heures moins le quart**". What time is that?

h. On the day of the excursion, breakfast is being served early, but you're not sure at what time. Ask.

i. How would you say in French:

i) meat	iv) fish	vii) ice cream	x) port
ii) steak	v) salmon	viii) pastry	
iii) duck	vi) trout	ix) wine	

j. Reply to these questions:

i) A quelle heure servez-vous le petit déjeuner?

ii) A quelle heure arrive le car?

iii) A quelle heure part le train?

FORGET-ME-NOT

French word	English association
l'ascenseur (*lift*)	ascend
en face de (*opposite*)	facing
la glace (*ice cream*)	glacier
le nom (*name*)	nomination

WORD LIST

MASCULINE NOUNS		FEMININE NOUNS	
l'apéritif	aperitif	la bibliothèque	library
l'ascenseur	lift	la boisson	drink
le bifteck (pron. beef-tek)	steak	la bouteille	bottle
le bureau	office	la carte	à la carte menu
le canard	duck	la cathédrale	cathedral
le car	coach	les crudités	certain vegetables,
le cinéma	cinema		served raw
le client	customer		as a starter
le dessert	dessert	l'essence	petrol
le fromage	cheese	la fenêtre	window
le légume	vegetable	la gare	station
le magasin	shop	l'heure	time, hour
le menu	menu	la librairie	bookshop
le nom	name	la pâtisserie	pastry
le pétrole	petroleum	la saison	season
le plateau	tray	la terrine	pâté
le poisson	fish	la truite	trout
le porto	port	la viande	meat
le saumon	salmon	la voiture	car
le tournedos	fillet steak		
le vin	wine		
le whisky	whisky		
commencer	to start	derrière	behind
demander	to ask (for)	devant	in front of
exiger	to demand	en face de	opposite
		ensuite	afterwards
à côté de	by, next to	par ici	this way
comme	like, as	par où?	which way?

 1. UN PLAN DE LA VILLE

    Tourist: Bonjour, Monsieur.
              Good morning/afternoon, Sir.

  Information: Bonjour, Madame.
              Good morning/afternoon, Madam.

    Tourist: Avez-vous un plan de la ville et un plan du métro, s'il vous plaît?
              Have you got a street map and an underground map, please?

  Information: Oui, Madame. Voilà.
              Yes, Madam. Here you are.

    Tourist: Merci. C'est combien?
               Thank you. How much is that?

  Information: Rien du tout. C'est gratuit.
              Nothing at all. It's free.

2. VOUS ÊTES LES BIENVENUS

Tourist: C'est notre premier séjour à Paris.
It's our first stay in Paris.

Information: Vous êtes les bienvenus!
Welcome!

Tourist: Merci. Qu'est-ce que nous pouvons visiter ici?
Thank you. What can we visit here?

Information: Eh bien, il faut aller voir la tour Eiffel, bien sûr. Il faut aussi visiter le Louvre, qui a été récemment agrandi, le musée d'Orsay avec ses collections de tableaux, et l'architecture particulière du Centre Georges-Pompidou.
Well, you must go and see the Eiffel Tower, of course. You must also visit the Louvre, which has recently been extended, the musée d'Orsay with its collections of paintings, and the unusual architecture of the Georges-Pompidou Centre.

3. QUASIMODO!

Information: Si vous avez le temps, vous pouvez descendre la Seine en bateau-mouche . . . et n'oubliez pas de visiter Notre-Dame et surtout de chercher Quasimodo!
If you have time, you can sail down the Seine on a cruise boat . . . and don't forget to visit Notre Dame and above all to look for Quasimodo!

INFORMATION

PLACES TO VISIT IN PARIS

La tour Eiffel

While in Paris, make sure you visit the Eiffel Tower with its breathtaking view over the city. The Tower, which is made of iron and rises to a height of 320 metres, was built by the French engineer Gustave Eiffel for the 1889 World Fair in Paris. Initially, it was considered by many to be an eyesore, but the Tower has now become a major tourist attraction.

Interestingly, the iron framework of the Statue of Liberty in New York was also designed by Eiffel. (Métro: Trocadéro, Bir-Hakeim.)

Notre-Dame de Paris
Started in 1163 and completed in 1345, this magnificent Gothic cathedral is a must on account of its superb architecture and splendid stained-glass windows. Napoleon's coronation took place here in 1804. The cathedral gave its name to a historical novel by Victor Hugo in 1831 (later made into a film), which featured a deformed hunched-back bellringer called Quasimodo. (Métro: Cité.)

Le musée d'Orsay
Until 1939 this art gallery was a bustling railway station! Today you can admire paintings by Monet, Renoir, Cézanne, Degas, Rousseau, Toulouse-Lautrec, and many others. Sculptures, architecture and photography from 1848 to 1914 are also on display. (Métro: Solférino.)

Le Centre Pompidou (Beaubourg)
Described by some as looking like a mass of scaffolding, by others as original and exciting, this cultural centre attracts 25,000 visitors daily. Opened in 1977, in the heart of Paris, it houses a vast library, modern art exhibitions, a cinema, a theatre, a language and dialect centre and an art bookshop. The centre was the brainchild of Georges Pompidou, who succeeded General de Gaulle as President of the French Republic in 1969. He was passionately fond of modern art. (Métro: Rambuteau.)

Le Musée du Louvre
This is the home of, amongst other masterpieces, the *Mona Lisa*, which the French call **La Joconde**. It is said to be the portrait of the wife of Francesco del Giocondo. The Louvre, formerly a royal palace, is now one of the largest and most famous museums in the world. In fact, it has been renamed the "**Grand Louvre**", as it has recently been enlarged and now offers an original combination of famous paintings, a cultural centre, conference rooms, vast car parks and – a high-class shopping area! (Métro: Louvre, Palais-Royal.)

GETTING AROUND PARIS
Le métro (the tube)

a) Find your destination on the underground map as you enter the **métro**, and then look for the name of the terminus of the line it is on – that's the name of the line you take.

b) It's cheaper to buy a booklet (**un carnet**) of ten tickets (about 45 francs).

c) If you need to change, look for the word "**Correspondance**" as you get out of the train. If you're leaving the station, look for "**Sortie**".

La SNCF (French Railways)

When you buy a railway ticket at a station (**une gare**), do make sure you date-stamp (**composter**) the ticket before getting on the train. You'll see special ticket-punching machines at the entrance to the platforms for this purpose. Failure to stamp your ticket could result in a fine.

Le RER (Regional Express Network)

Le Réseau Express Régional is a high-speed train service operating within Paris and out to Roissy-Charles-de-Gaulle and Orly airports and the suburbs.

LANGUAGE NOTES

MAPS

A street map is "**un plan de la ville**" and an underground map "**un plan du métro**", but a road map is "**une carte routière**".

COMBIEN?

"**Combien?**" means "How much?" or "How many?" You can ask "**C'est combien?**" instead of "**Quel est le prix . . . ?**"
When "**combien**" is used with a noun, "**de**" is inserted:

Combien de sucre? (*How much sugar?*)
Combien de billets? (*How many tickets?*)

FREE

"**Gratuit**" means "free of charge", but the French for "free" meaning "not busy" or "independent" is "**libre**".

Je suis libre ce soir. (*I'm free this evening.*)

GOING UP AND DOWN

The basic meaning of "**descendre**" is "to go/come/bring down". For instance:

Vous pouvez descendre la Seine. (*You can go down the Seine.*)
Voulez-vous descendre les bagages? (*Would you bring down the luggage?*)

The opposite of "**descendre**" is "**monter**" (*to go/come/bring up*):

Je vais monter. (*I'll go up.*)

EN BATEAU-MOUCHE

"**Le bateau**" is a boat. "**La mouche**" is a fly. The name "**bateau-mouche**" may have been coined for the boats providing sightseeing trips on the Seine, because of their glass roofs which make them resemble a fly.

QU'EST-CE QUE . . . ?

This might look complicated, but it is simple to pronounce (kess-ker) and simple to use. It means "What . . . ?", as in:

Qu'est-ce que vous désirez manger? (*What would you like to eat?*)
Qu'est-ce que vous cherchez? (*What are you looking for?*)
Qu'est-ce que nous pouvons visiter? (*What can we visit?*)
Qu'est-ce que c'est? (*What is this/that?*)

SOME MORE QUESTION WORDS

Où? (*Where?*)   **Où habitez-vous?** (*Where do you live?*)
Quand? (*When?*)   **Quand partez-vous?** (*When are you leaving?*)

47

Pourquoi? (*Why?*) **Pourquoi aimez-vous Paris?** (*Why do you like Paris?*)

Comment? (*How?*) **Comment allez-vous?** (*How are you? - literally, How do you go?*)

Qui? (*Who?*) **Qui est l'architecte?** (*Who is the architect?*)

TO BE ABLE – POUVOIR

The tourist asked **"Qu'est-ce que nous pouvons visiter?"** **"Pouvons"** comes from the verb **"pouvoir"**, which has an irregular pattern:

je peux (*I can*)	**nous pouvons** (*we can*)
vous pouvez (*you can*)	
il/elle peut (*he/she/it can*)	**ils/elles peuvent** (*they can*)

Here are some examples:

Elle peut louer une voiture. (*She can hire a car.*)
Vous pouvez visiter Versailles. (*You can visit Versailles.*)
Est-ce que je peux téléphoner? (*Can I telephone?*)

"Pourriez-vous . . . ?" (*Could you . . . ?*), which we met on page 20, is another form of the verb **"pouvoir"**.

IL FAUT

This expression can be used for "I/You/He/She/It/We/They must . . . " The exact meaning depends on the context.

Il faut réserver une table. (*I/We/You etc must reserve a table.*)
Il faut demander une chambre près de l'ascenseur. (*We/You/They etc must ask for a room near the lift.*)

"Il faut" can be used in another way too. Look at these examples:

Il nous faut de l'argent français. (*We need some French money.*)
Il faut deux minutes pour aller au théâtre. (*It takes – or I/We/They etc need – two minutes to get to the theatre.*)

You can see, perhaps, that **"il faut"** literally means something like "it is needed".

QUI – WHO/WHICH

The little word "**qui**" means "who" or "which", as for example in:

le guide qui parle anglais (*the guide who speaks English*)
l'autocar qui va à l'aéroport (*the coach which goes to the airport*)

WHO? AND WHICH?

"Who?" is "**Qui?**":

Qui est l'architecte de cette église? (*Who is the architect of this church?*)

"Which . . . ?" is "**Quel?/Quelle?/Quels?/Quelles . . . ?**", as in "**Quelle excursion?**" (*Which excursion?*). To revise this, see pages 19 and 30.

SI

This little word has two meanings. It means "if" as in:

Si vous avez le temps, visitez la cathédrale. (*If you have time, visit the cathedral.*)

It is also used instead of "**oui**" as an emphatic "yes", in reply to a negative question. For instance:

Vous ne mangez pas ici? (*Aren't you eating here?*)
Si! (*Oh yes!*)

N'OUBLIEZ PAS "NE . . . PAS"!

You know that "not" is expressed in French by putting "**ne**" before the verb and "**pas**" after it (see page 30). But if the verb begins with a vowel or an "h", "**ne**" is contracted to "**n'**":

N'oubliez pas . . . (*Don't forget . . .*)
Je n'ai pas acheté de timbres. (*I have not bought any stamps.*)
Nous n'habitons pas à Londres. (*We don't live in London.*)

DE

In different contexts, "**de**" means different things (see overleaf). You know it means "of", as in "**le plan de la ville**" (*map of the town*) and "**le plan du métro**" (*map of the underground*). Remember how "**de**" plus "**le**" form "**du**" (page 39).

Here are some examples of "**de**" with a range of meanings:

of: **la chambre de ma fille** (*my daughter's room*, literally, *the room of my daughter*)

from: **J'ai reçu un fax de ma secrétaire.** (*I have received a fax from my secretary.*)

to: **N'oubliez pas de chercher Quasimodo!** (*Don't forget to look for Quasimodo!*)

any: **Nous n'avons pas de thé.** (*We haven't any tea.*)

SOME MORE NUMBERS

21	**vingt et un**	26	**vingt-six**
22	**vingt-deux**	27	**vingt-sept**
23	**vingt-trois**	28	**vingt-huit**
24	**vingt-quatre**	29	**vingt-neuf**
25	**vingt-cinq**	30	**trente**

YOUR TURN

1. WHERE'S THE TOURIST INFORMATION OFFICE?
Ask that lady over there where the tourist information office is. She replies: "**Allez tout droit, Monsieur. Le syndicat d'initiative est juste derrière la cathédrale.**" Check your answer with the key on page 102.

2. COULD YOU COPE IN THE TOURIST OFFICE?
If you can, use the tape to practise taking part in the following conversation with the clerk in the tourist information office. Check your part against the key on page 102.

You: Good morning. Do you have a street map of Paris?

Clerk: **Oui, Monsieur . . . Voilà.**

You: Thank you. Where can I hire a car? When can we visit Versailles? Which excursions do you recommend? How can we go to the Eiffel Tower? Where can I telephone?

(You are given various leaflets and you get all the information you need.)

Clerk: **Je vous recommande aussi de descendre la Seine en bateau-mouche.**

3. BACK AT THE HOTEL
Now take part in this conversation:

You: Excuse me. Where can I buy some stamps?
Receptionist: **Il faut aller à la poste, Madame, ou dans un bureau de tabac . . . Vous êtes Madame Green, non?**
You: Yes, that's right.
Receptionist: **Nous avons reçu ce matin un fax de votre secrétaire.**
You: A fax? From my secretary?
Receptionist: **Oui. Un instant . . . Voilà le fax.**
You: Thank you very much . . . Good heavens! I've forgotten to pay her!

4. FAST NUMBERS
Say these numbers fast in French. Check yourself with the tape if you can.
29 19 9 30 21 26 14 7 11

FORGET-ME-NOT

French word	English association
aller (*to go*)	alley
l'argent (*money*)	Argentina (land of silver)
chercher (*to look for*)	search
gratuit (*free of charge*)	gratis
habiter (*to live*)	inhabit
libre (*free*)	liberty
monter (*to go up*)	mount
le séjour (*stay*)	sojourn
le temps (*time*)	temporary
la ville (*town*)	village
voir (*to see*)	voyeur

WORD LIST

MASCULINE NOUNS		FEMININE NOUNS	
l'aéroport	airport	l'architecture	architecture
l'architecte	architect	la carte routière	road map
l'argent	money	la collection	collection
l'autocar	coach	l'église	church
les bagages	luggage	l'excursion	excursion
le bateau	boat	la plage	beach
le fax	fax	la secrétaire	secretary
le guide	guide	la ville	town
le métro	underground		
le musée	museum		
le plan	plan, map		
le séjour	stay		
le sucre	sugar		
le syndicat d'initiative	tourist information office		
le tableau	picture		
le temps	time		
le théâtre	theatre		
le timbre	stamp		

agrandir	to enlarge	combien?	how many?, how much?
aller	to go		
chercher	to look for	comment?	how?
descendre	to go down	gratuit	free (costing nothing)
habiter	to live		
monter	to go up, climb	libre	free
oublier	to forget	pourquoi?	why?
partir	to leave, depart	premier (fem. première)	first
pouvoir	to be able	quand?	when?
recevoir	to receive	qu'est-ce que . . . ?	what . . . ?
visiter	to visit	qui?	who?
voir	to see	qui	who, which
		récemment	recently
		rien	nothing

7 A Lost Bag

Suppose you left your travel bag in a restaurant and, although you went back only ten minutes later, it had disappeared. You would need to report the loss to the police. So go along to the nearest police station (**le commissariat de police**).

 1. NOUS AVONS OUBLIÉ NOTRE SAC

Tourist: Bonsoir, Monsieur. Nous avons oublié notre sac de voyage dans un restaurant et il a disparu.
Good evening. We left our travel bag in a restaurant and it has disappeared.

Police officer: Quel est le nom du restaurant, Madame?
What's the name of the restaurant, Madam?

Tourist: "Brèves Rencontres".
"Brief Encounters".

Police officer: Quand êtes-vous allés au restaurant?
When did you go to the restaurant?

Tourist: Aujourd'hui, mercredi.
Today, Wednesday.

Police officer: Aujourd'hui . . . le treize août. Et à quelle heure êtes-vous arrivés?
Today . . . the 13th August. And at what time did you arrive?

Tourist: À une heure et demie.
At one thirty.

Police officer: À quelle heure êtes-vous partis?
At what time did you leave?

Tourist: À trois heures.
At three o'clock.

2. VOUS AVEZ UNE ADRESSE ICI?

Police officer: Vous avez une adresse ici à Paris?
Do you have an address here in Paris?

Tourist: Oui. Voici l'adresse de notre hôtel.
Yes. Here's the address of our hotel.

Police officer: Vous connaissez le numéro de téléphone?
Do you know the telephone number?

Tourist: Oui . . . Vingt-cinq, dix-neuf, trente et un, onze.
Yes . . . Twenty-five, nineteen, thirty-one, eleven.

Police officer: Merci. Quand êtes-vous arrivés en France?
Thank you. When did you arrive in France?

Tourist: Il y a trois jours.
Three days ago.

Police officer: Combien de temps allez-vous rester?
How long are you going to stay?

Tourist: À Paris? Environ une semaine.
In Paris? About one week.

Police officer: Quelle est votre profession?
What's your profession?

Tourist: Je suis journaliste.
I'm a journalist.

3. POUVEZ-VOUS DÉCRIRE LE SAC?

Police officer: Pouvez-vous décrire le sac et le contenu?
Can you describe the bag and its contents?

Tourist: Le sac est assez grand . . . avec deux petits trous sur le côté.
The bag is quite big . . . with two small holes in the side.

Police officer: Deux petits trous? Ah bon? Et qu'est-ce qu'il y a dedans?
Two small holes? Really? And what is there inside?

Tourist: De l'argent . . . environ mille francs, des chèques de voyage, un appareil-photo, des clés, une petite boîte de "ron-ron" et . . . un . . . chat.
Some money . . . about 1000 francs, some traveller's cheques, a camera, some keys, a small tin of "ron-ron" and . . . a . . . cat.

Police officer: Un chat?
A cat?

Tourist: Oui. C'est affreux! . . . Nous sommes prêts à offrir une récompense.
Yes. It's terrible! . . . We are prepared to offer a reward.

4. DE QUELLE COULEUR?

Police officer: De quelle couleur est le sac?
What colour is the bag?

Tourist: Il est rouge.
It's red.

Police officer: De quelle couleur est le chat?
What colour is the cat?

Tourist: Il est blanc . . . avec une patte noire. Il s'appelle César. Il est très affectueux.
He's white . . . with a black paw. He's called Caesar. He's very affectionate.

Police officer: Bien. Je vais vous contacter à votre hôtel le plus vite possible.
OK. I'll contact you at your hotel as soon as possible.

INFORMATION

FRENCH POLICE

Les agents de police

Most English-speaking people believe that the French word for "policeman" is **"gendarme"**, but this is only partly correct. If, while staying in France, you lose your camera or wallet, or they are stolen, or if your car is broken into, etc, you should go along to the **commissariat de police**, where an **agent de police** will be on duty to help and advise you.

Les gendarmes

Should you find yourself in difficulty in a rural area, there won't be a **commissariat de police** and you'll need to deal with the local **gendarmerie**, where you'll explain your problem to a **gendarme**. The **gendarmerie** is, in fact, part of the army.

Les CRS

You've probably read English newspaper reports of the CRS being called out to deal with demonstrations and riots by French students and farmers. The CRS (**Compagnie républicaine de sécurité**) are the state security police and are also responsible for the safety of VIPs such as heads of state, ministers, famous visitors, etc.

Les agents contractuels

Un contractuel (**-elle**, f.) is a "traffic warden" and part of the police. The French sometimes refer to the lady traffic wardens, informally, as "**les pervenches**" – i.e. periwinkles (small blue flowers) because of the colour of their uniforms.

LANGUAGE NOTES

MONTHS AND DAYS

You will need to know how to say the months of the year:

janvier (jahng-vyay)	**juillet** (jü'ee-yay)
février (fay-vree-yay)	**août** (oot)
mars (mahrr-ss)	**septembre** (sep-tahng-br)
avril (ah-vreel)	**octobre** (ok-to-br)
mai (may)	**novembre** (no-vahng-br)
juin (jü'ang)	**décembre** (day-sahng-br)

And the days of the week, starting with Monday:

lundi (lerng-dee)	**vendredi** (vahng-drer-dee)
mardi (mahrr-dee)	**samedi** (sahm-dee)
mercredi (mairr-krer-dee)	**dimanche** (dee-mahng-sh)
jeudi (jer-dee)	

DATES

In English we say "the second of January", "the third of August", "the fourth . . . ", etc. The French say "the two January", "the three August" :

le deux janvier   **le trois août**   **le treize août**

TELEPHONE NUMBERS

In France, telephone numbers are divided into groups of two. For instance, "22 17 35" (**vingt-deux, dix-sept, trente-cinq**).

THIRTY-ONE TO FIFTY

31	**trente et un**	41	**quarante et un**
32	**trente-deux**	43	**quarante-trois**
35	**trente-cinq**	44	**quarante-quatre**
39	**trente-neuf**	48	**quarante-huit**
40	**quarante**	50	**cinquante**

COLOURS

Here's a palette of colours for you to learn:

red	**rouge**	brown	**marron**	grey	**gris**
yellow	**jaune**	green	**vert**	black	**noir**
blue	**bleu**	pink	**rose**	white	**blanc**

In the following examples, note the word order:

du vin rouge (*some red wine*)
une robe jaune (*a yellow dress*)
une chemise bleue (*a blue shirt*)

The colour words that don't already end in "e" (like "**bleu**") gain an "e" when they are used to describe a feminine noun; "**blanc**" in the feminine becomes "**blanche**". "**Marron**" (*brown*) is invariable.

C'EST AFFREUX!

This means "It's dreadful!" Hopefully, on your trip to France, you might have more use for the first two in this list:

C'est bien. (*It's fine.*)
C'est bon. (*It's good./It's tasty.*)

C'est important. (*It's important.*)
C'est très grave. (*It's very serious.*)
C'est urgent. (*It's urgent.*)
Ce n'est pas bon. (*It's not good./It doesn't taste good.*)
Ce n'est pas important. (*It's not important.*)

OCCUPATIONS

When the French talk about what they do for a living, they omit "a/an", for instance:

Je suis acteur. (*I'm an actor.*)
Elle est dentiste. (*She's a dentist.*)
Elle est journaliste. (*She's a journalist.*)
Il est professeur. (*He's a teacher.*)

JE M'APPELLE ...

Someone might ask you "**Comment vous appelez-vous?**" (*What are you called?* or *What is your name?*). So learn the expression: "**Je m'appelle** [your name]."

To say "He/She is called . . . ", learn "**Il/Elle s'appelle . . .** "

DÉCRIRE AND ÉCRIRE

"**Décrire**" means "to describe", as in "**Pouvez-vous décrire le sac?**"

A very similar-sounding word, "**écrire**", means "to write". For instance, "**Voulez-vous écrire l'adresse, s'il vous plaît?**" (*Would you write the address, please?*)

JE CONNAIS, VOUS CONNAISSEZ

The policeman asked "**Vous connaissez le numéro de téléphone?**" (*Do you know the telephone number?*) "I know" is "**Je connais**". Here are some more examples:

Je ne connais pas son nom. (*I don't know his/her name.*)
Vous connaissez Paris. (*You know Paris.*)

QUITE ENOUGH!

"**Le sac est assez grand**" – "*the bag is quite big*"; in this case, "**assez**" means "quite" or "fairly".

The word for "very" is "**très**" ("**Le sac est très grand**") and the word for "extremely" is "**extrêmement**" ("**Le sac est extrêmement grand**").

"**Assez**" also means "enough": for instance, in this sentence:

Je n'ai pas assez d'argent. (*I haven't enough money.*)

RESTER (TO STAY)

This French word is another false friend! It doesn't mean "to rest", as you might think, but "to stay, to remain". "To rest" is "**se reposer**".

RONRONNER (TO PURR)

The lost bag contained "**une boîte de 'ron-ron'**". It is a popular brand of cat food in France.

IL Y A

This useful expression has two separate meanings. First it can mean "There is . . . " or "There are . . . ", as in:

Il y a une erreur dans l'addition. (*There's a mistake in the bill.*)

Second, it can mean "ago" as in:

Nous sommes arrivés en France il y a une semaine. (*We arrived in France one week ago.*)

NOUS SOMMES ARRIVÉS

We have seen that, to talk about the past in French, we normally need to use the verb "**avoir**" followed by a word like "**parlé**" or "**demandé**" or "**choisi**" (see pages 38-39).

"**Arriver**" (*to arrive*), however, has a different form in the past. It and three other important verbs, "**venir**" (*to come*), "**aller**" (*to go*) and "**partir**" (*to leave*), use the verb "**être**", instead of "**avoir**", in the past. Look carefully at the examples overleaf:

Je suis arrivé. (*I arrived./I have arrived.*)
Je suis venu. (*I came./I have come.*)
Je suis allé. (*I went.*)
Je suis parti. (*I left.*)

Literally, these mean, not "I <u>have</u> arrived", for instance, but "I <u>am</u> arrived".

In the case of these four exceptional verbs which make their past with "**être**", the words "**arrivé**", "**venu**", etc, change their endings, as follows:

je suis arrivé (if "**je**" is male)
je suis arrivée (if "**je**" is female)
il est arrivé
elle est arrivée
nous sommes arrivés (or **arrivées**, if all female)
vous êtes arrivé (or **arrivée** if female,
    or **arrivés** if several people)
ils sont arrivés
elles sont arriveés

There are other verbs which follow the same pattern.

LE SAC A DISPARU

This is one other exception to notice. Most verbs in the past change their ending to "**-é**" – like "**j'ai invité**" (*I invited*), "**j'ai aidé**" (*I helped*), "**j'ai demandé . . .** " (*I asked for . . .*). However, a small number of verbs such as "**disparaître**" (*to disappear*) end in "**u**" – "**Le sac a disparu**".

YOUR TURN

1.COULD YOU COPE?
a. Tell the police officer that the following items have
   disappeared:
   i) your umbrella   iii) your briefcase
   ii) your wife's new dress iv) your watch
b. Tell the hotel receptionist that your camera has disappeared
   from your room.

c. Say to French friends you have recently made: "We arrived in France a week ago."

d. Say the following dates in French:
   i) 3rd January   iii) 31st August
   ii) 24th February   iv) 16th November

e. Say this telephone number in French: 19 44 25 33 01.

f. Mention four occupations in French.

g. Imagine you have filled in a form to hire a car and realize that you have completed the wrong section. The clerk says "**Ce n'est pas grave**." What does this mean?

h. Your suitcase has been mislaid by the airline. Describe it as follows: It's red, it's large. Inside there are shirts, dresses, books, shoes, a blue vanity case.

i. A French acquaintance asks "**Combien de temps allez-vous rester en France?**" Does this mean:
   i) Have you come to France for a rest?
   ii) How much are you going to spend in France?
   iii) How long are you going to stay in France?

 2. AT THE LOST PROPERTY OFFICE
Take part in the following conversation, using the tape if you can. You can check your part with the key on page 103.

You: Can you help me? I've left a bag on the underground.
Official: **Quel jour et à quelle heure, Madame?**
You: Yesterday, Friday. At half past three.
Official: **Entre quelles stations?**
You: Between Concorde and Opéra.
Official: **Pouvez-vous décrire le sac?**
You: It's fairly large, it's white, and there's a picture of the Eiffel Tower on the side.
Official: **Qu'est-ce qu'il y a dedans?**
You: A beautiful dressing gown. I bought it for my husband.
Official: **Cette robe de chambre, elle est jaune, rouge, verte et rose?**
You: Yes, that's right! Have you found the dressing gown?
Official: **Oui. La voici.**
You: Oh, thank you very much. It's beautiful, isn't it?
Official: **Euh . . . oui . . . euh . . . C'est une question de goût.**

61

FORGET-ME-NOT

French word	English association
blanc (*white*)	blank
je connais (*I know*)	connoisseur
écrire (*to write*)	scribe (initial "é" in French often becomes "s" in English)
jaune (*yellow*)	jaundice
venir (*to come*)	venue
vert (*green*)	verdure

WORD LIST

MASCULINE NOUNS		FEMININE NOUNS	
l'acteur	actor	**l'adresse**	address
l'agent de police	policeman	**la boîte**	box; tin, can
l'appareil-photo	camera	**la chemise**	shirt
le boulanger	baker	**la clé**	key
le chèque de voyage	traveller's cheque	**la couleur**	colour
le commissariat de police	police station	**l'erreur**	error, mistake
le contenu	contents	**la patte**	paw
le dentiste	dentist	**la profession**	profession,
le gendarme	country policeman		occupation
le journaliste	journalist	**la récompense**	reward
le médecin	doctor	**la robe**	dress
le plombier	plumber		
le professeur	teacher		
le trou	hole		
aider	to help	**affectueux**	affectionate
s'appeler	to be called	**assez**	quite, fairly
connaître	to know	**dedans**	inside
contacter	to contact	**environ**	around, about
décrire	to describe	**extrêmement**	extremely
disparaître	to disappear	**grave**	serious
écrire	to write	**il y a**	there is/are; ago
inviter	to invite	**important**	important
offrir	to offer	**prêt**	ready
se reposer	to rest	**très**	very
rester	to stay	**urgent**	urgent
venir	to come	**vite**	quickly

8 Travelling by Car

Now imagine that you have hired a car and are travelling along the motorway, en route to Lyon. First you need to stop at a petrol station; and next (dialogue 4), having seen road signs announcing **"Péage 700m"** (*Toll 700m*) and **"Préparez 20F"** (*Have ready 20F*), you stop at a tollbooth.

 1. LE PLEIN, S'IL VOUS PLAÎT

Tourist: Bonjour, Monsieur.

Attendant: Bonjour, Madame.

Tourist: Le plein de sans plomb, s'il vous plaît.
Fill it up with unleaded, please.

Attendant: Oui, Madame . . . Voilà.
Yes, Madam . . . There you are.

Tourist: Merci. C'est combien?
Thank you. How much is that?

Attendant: Deux cents francs. Voulez-vous payer à la

caisse, s'il vous plaît?
Two hundred francs. Would you pay at the cashdesk, please?

Tourist: Oui, d'accord.
Yes, OK.

2. L'ESSENCE

Attendant: Est-ce que l'essence est moins chère en Angleterre?
Is petrol cheaper in England?

Tourist: Oui, un peu.
Yes, a little.

Attendant: L'essence en France est peut-être de meilleure qualité?
Perhaps the petrol in France is better quality?

Tourist: Peut-être . . . Voulez-vous vérifier l'huile, s'il vous plaît, et la pression des pneus? Et pouvez-vous nettoyer le pare-brise?
Perhaps . . . Please would you check the oil, and the tyre pressures? And can you clean the windscreen?

3. ATTENTION AU BROUILLARD!

Attendant: Voilà. C'est fait. Bonne route! Attention au brouillard! . . . Il nous arrive d'Angleterre!
There you are. That's done. Have a good journey! Watch out for the fog! . . . It's coming from England!

4. NOUS N'AVONS PAS DE MONNAIE

Tourist: Excusez-moi, Monsieur, mais nous n'avons pas de monnaie. Nous avons seulement un billet de cent francs.
I'm sorry, but we haven't any change. We have only a hundred franc note.

Toll attendant: Pas de problème, Madame. Voici votre monnaie: cinquante, soixante, soixante-dix, quatre-vingts francs . . . Attention! Votre ceinture n'est pas attachée et la police de la route n'est pas loin.
No problem, Madam. Here's your change: fifty,

> *sixty, seventy, eighty francs . . . . Be careful! Your seat belt isn't fastened and the traffic police aren't far away.*

Tourist: Ah bon? Merci beaucoup. Mais la ceinture est trop courte pour moi . . .
> *Really? Thank you very much. But the belt is too short for me . . .*

Toll attendant: Et, en plus, c'est très dangereux!
> *And, furthermore, it's very dangerous!*

Tourist: Oui. Je sais.
> *Yes. I know.*

INFORMATION

DRIVING IN FRANCE

French drivers are not as bad as some rumours would have you believe! Just remember to drive on the right (**à droite**) and in built-up areas to give way (**la priorité**) to traffic coming from the right, unless there's an indication to the contrary. By law you must have in your car a warning triangle, in case of accident, and a set of replacement bulbs.

*Petrol (**l'essence**)*
As in Britain, petrol prices vary from pump to pump, and depending on the grade. The grades of petrol are called: **super** (4-*star*); **sans plomb** (*unleaded*); and **super sans plomb** (*unleaded super plus*). ("**Sans plomb**" literally means "without lead".)

*Toll motorways (**les autoroutes à péage**)*
On most French motorways you'll have to pay a toll. It can, actually, work out quite expensive to cross France from one end to the other, but, on the other hand, you'll save a great deal of time, as French motorways are much less congested than British ones. To give you an idea of the cost, if you drive on the A13 between Caen and Rouen, 120 kilometres, you'll have to pay 34 francs.

*The highway code (**le code de la route**)*
Nowadays most traffic signs are international. As regards roundabouts, sometimes the traffic on the roundabout gives way and sometimes it doesn't. This is because the French are beginning to adopt the principle of "**le rond-point anglais**" (*the English roundabout*), where traffic approaching does not have right of way. When this is the case, you'll see a sign saying "**Vous n'avez pas la priorité**". Other important instructions you must understand are "**Cédez le passage**" (*Give way*) and "**passage protégé**" (*you have priority*).

*Speed limits (**limitations de vitesse**)*
In France the maximum speed limits are:

On toll motorways	130 km/hour
On free motorways and dual carriageways	110 km/hour
On other roads	90 km/hour
In built-up areas	50 km/hour

*Road tax disc (**la vignette**)*
It may interest you to know that, every year, before 31st December, all French drivers must purchase a new **vignette**. The cost varies according to the age of the car and the power of the engine.

For more details about safe driving in France, you should consult the various publications of the AA and the RAC.

*The MOT (**le contrôle technique**)*
Until very recently cars in France, no matter how old, did not have to submit to any form of mechanical inspection. Since 1st January 1994, however, a **contrôle technique** has been introduced for cars over five years old, and soon maybe four years. The cost for inspection is 300F and an official sticker (**le macaron**) proving that the test has taken place must be displayed on the windscreen.

Bonne route!

LANGUAGE NOTES

LE PLEIN DE SANS PLOMB – "FAIRE"

"**Le plein**" is an abbreviation for a command, "**Faites le plein**" (literally, *"Do the full"*).

"**Faites**" is part of the irregular verb "**faire**" (*to do* or *to make*). When the petrol pump attendant says "**C'est fait**" (*That's done*), he is using the past of "**faire**". "I have done" is "**j'ai fait**".

COMPARISONS

In French, when you want to make comparisons, you use "**plus**" (pronounced "plü"), meaning "more", or "**moins**" (pronounced "mwang"), meaning "less". "Than" is expressed by "**que**" (pronounced "ker") or "**qu'**", before a vowel. Here are some examples:

Le train est plus rapide que la voiture. (*The train is faster than the car.*)
Le film est moins intéressant que le livre. (*The film is less interesting than the book.*)
L'essence est moins chère en Angleterre? (*Is petrol cheaper in England?*)

GOOD AND BETTER

"Good" in French is "**bon**" (or "**bonne**" in the feminine). In English we don't say "gooder" and the French don't say "plus bon". The English is "better" and the French is "**meilleur**" (or "**meilleure**" in the feminine).

BONNE ROUTE!

This means "Have a good journey!" You may also like to learn some other expressions with "**bon**" or "**bonne**":

Bon anniversaire! (*Happy birthday!*)
Bon appétit! (*Enjoy your meal!*)
Bon courage! (*Take heart!*)

Bon voyage! (*Have a good trip!*)
Bon week-end! (*Have a good weekend!*)

Bonne Année! (*Happy New Year!*)
Bonne chance! (*Good luck!*)
Bonne journée! (*Have a good day!*)
Bonne santé! (*Keep well!*)

ATTENTION!

"**Attention!**" means "Be careful!" If you want to say "Beware of" (or "Mind") something, use "**Attention à ...!**" For instance:

Attention à la marche! (*Mind the step!*)

COUNTRIES

England	l'Angleterre	Japan	le Japon
France	la France	Russia	la Russie
Germany	l'Allemagne	Spain	l'Espagne
Italy	l'Italie	United States	les États-Unis

"IT"

In French, "it" is either "**il**" or "**elle**". For instance, the petrol station attendant said: "**Il nous arrive d'Angleterre**" (*It's coming to us from England*). "It" was the fog, "**le brouillard**" (masculine), so "it" in this case is "**il**".

If, when you are speaking French, you want to say something about "it" but you cannot remember whether the word you're referring to is masculine or feminine, use "**C'est**" instead, with the masculine – for instance, "**C'est bon**" (*It's good*).

TOO MUCH, TOO MANY

"**Très**" is "very". "**Trop**" is "too", as in:

C'est très dangereux. (*It's very dangerous.*)
C'est trop dangereux. (*It's too dangerous.*)

"**Trop de**" means "too much" or "too many":

Nous avons acheté trop de pain. (*We've bought too much bread.*)

SOME MONEY WORDS

Make sure you don't confuse "**la monnaie**" (*small change*) with "**l'argent**" (*money*).

A bank note is "**un billet**" – the same word as is used for "a ticket". But the context will always make it clear which meaning is intended.

JE CONNAIS OR JE SAIS?

You have learnt that "I know" in French is "**je connais**" (page 58). But, when the tourist in dialogue 4 says she <u>knows</u> it is dangerous not to wear her seat belt, she says "**je sais**". "**Je connais**" is used for knowing (being familiar with) places and persons. "**Je sais**" is used for knowing a fact. For example:

Je connais Paris. (*I know Paris.*)
Je sais où est Paris. (*I know where Paris is.*)

SIXTY TO EIGHTY

60	**soixante**	72	**soixante-douze**
61	**soixante et un**	73	**soixante-treize**
67	**soixante-sept**	74	**soixante-quatorze**
70	**soixante-dix**	79	**soixante-dix-neuf**
71	**soixante et onze**	80	**quatre-vingts**

YOUR TURN

1. COULD YOU COPE?

a. You've pulled in at a petrol station. Greet the attendant and ask him to fill up the tank.

b. The attendant says: "**Super? Sans plomb? Super sans plomb?**" Ask for 4-star petrol.

c. Ask him to check the water.

d. Tell him to mind the radiator – it's very hot!

e. Ask if you have to pay at the cashdesk.

f. Comment on the weather: say it's raining heavily. Add that the rain is probably coming from Spain.

g. You're at the tollbooth. Apologise for not having any change.

h. Add that you have only a 200F note.

 2. A ROUTINE CHECK

Take part in the following dialogue, using the tape if you can. You can check your part with the key on page 103. A French police motorcyclist has just signalled to you to pull over.

Officer: **Bonjour, Madame . . . Monsieur. Vous avez vos papiers, s'il vous plaît?**

You: I'm sorry. I don't understand.

Officer: **Votre permis de conduire** (*driving licence*)**, votre assurance, votre carte grise** (*registration document*)**, s'il vous plaît.**

You: Oh, now I understand. Yes, of course. I'm sorry. Here you are, Officer.

Officer: **Mais où est la photo?**

You: We don't have photos in England.

Officer: **C'est votre voiture?**

You: No. We hired the car this morning.

Officer: **Où allez-vous?**

You: We're going to Lyon.

Officer: **D'où venez-vous?**

You: From Paris.

Officer: **C'est parfait. C'est simplement un contrôle de routine. Bonne route!**

You: Phew! I had a narrow escape with my belt!

FORGET-ME-NOT

French word	English association
court (*short*)	curtail
meilleur (*better*)	ameliorate
le pare-brise (*windscreen*)	breeze
plein (*full*)	replenish, plenty
le pneu (*tyre*)	pneumatic

WORD LIST

MASCULINE NOUNS

l'anniversaire	birthday
l'appétit	appetite
le billet	banknote; ticket
le brouillard	fog
le courage	courage
le film	film
le livre	book
le pain	bread
le pare-brise	windscreen
le péage	toll
le pneu	tyre
le problème	problem
le train	train
le week-end	weekend

FEMININE NOUNS

l'année	year
la caisse	cashdesk
la chance	luck
l'eau	water
l'huile	oil
la journée	day
la monnaie	small change
la police	the police
la pression	pressure
la route	road
la santé	health
la station-service	petrol station

faire	to do, to make
nettoyer	to clean
savoir	to know (a fact)

bon marché	cheap
cher	dear, expensive
court	short
dangereux	dangerous
de bonne qualité	good-quality
en sécurité	safe
intéressant	interesting
lent	slow
loin	far
un peu	a little
peut-être	perhaps
plein	full
rapide	fast

D'accord!	OK!, Right!
Pas de problème!	No problem!
Ma voiture est en panne	My car has broken down

9 Arriving at your Gîte

You have arrived at your destination – Pontèves, in Provence – and find the small house on a hill, which you have rented, about a kilometre from the village. The owner, M. Blanchet, is expecting you.

 1. VENEZ VISITER LA MAISON

> *Owner:* Vous êtes bien Monsieur et Madame Green?
> *You must be Mr and Mrs Green?*
>
> *Tourist:* Oui, c'est ça, Monsieur.
> *Yes. That's right.*
>
> *Owner:* Bienvenue à Pontèves! Je suis Monsieur Blanchet. Entrez. Venez visiter la maison.
> *Welcome to Pontèves! I'm Monsieur Blanchet. Come in. Come and see the house.*
>
> *Tourist:* Merci, Monsieur.
> *Thank you.*

2. C'EST PARFAIT!

Tourist: Quelle belle salle de séjour! . . . La cuisine est bien équipée.
What a beautiful living room! . . . The kitchen is well equipped.

Owner: La chambre donne sur le jardin.
The bedroom looks out onto the garden.

Tourist: Oui. C'est parfait. Où est-ce que nous pouvons faire nos courses?
Yes. It's perfect. Where can we do our shopping?

Owner: Vous pouvez acheter les fruits, les légumes et les œufs à la ferme à côté, ou au marché du village.
You can buy fruit, vegetables and eggs at the farm nearby, or in the village market.

3. LE TOURISME ET LES DISTRACTIONS

Tourist: Et pour le tourisme? Qu'est-ce que vous recommandez?
And what about sight-seeing? What do you recommend?

Owner: D'abord notre village, avec les ruines du château, puis les lacs, les vallées, et la ville de Fréjus qui est très ancienne. Elle date du douzième siècle.
First of all our village, with the castle ruins, then the lakes, and the valleys, and the town of Fréjus, which is very old. It dates from the twelfth century.

Tourist: Et pour les distractions?
And what about entertainment?

Owner: Il y a les fêtes locales, les bals populaires, les promenades en montagne, les sports nautiques sur la côte, les petits restaurants . . . La spécialité de la région, c'est la bouillabaisse.
There are local celebrations, village dances, hiking in the mountains, water sports on the coast, little restaurants . . . The speciality of the region is bouillabaisse.

4. LA BOUILLABAISSE

Tourist: La bouillabaisse, qu'est-ce que c'est?
What is bouillabaisse?

Owner: Une excellente soupe de poissons avec une sauce à l'ail.
An excellent fish soup with a garlic sauce.

Tourist: A l'ail? . . . Aïe, aïe!
Garlic? . . . Oh dear!

INFORMATION

GÎTES

A **gîte** can be translated as "self-catering holiday accommodation" but there's far more to this kind of holiday than that. You will stay in a flat, a cottage, or a renovated farmhouse and these are often to be found in small villages or on farms.

The great attraction of renting a **gîte** is that you'll be able to enjoy the beauty of the French countryside and let the children run free in large open spaces, close to the animals on the farm. You'll be able to buy most of what you need from the village shops and from the farmers, and to chat with them (in French, of course) about your respective lifestyles and, no doubt, solve together all the international problems of the day.

Accommodation in a **gîte** tends to be fairly simple, but standards of quality are laid down by the **Fédération Nationale des Gîtes Ruraux de France**. You can obtain free brochures, giving details of both **Gîtes** and **Logis de France** from: Gîtes de France Ltd, 178 Piccadilly, London W1V 9DB.

Useful words
Household items

sheet	**le drap**	washing powder	**la lessive**
blanket	**la couverture**	vacuum cleaner	**l'aspirateur**
pillow	**l'oreiller**	shutters	**les volets**
pillowcase	**la taie d'oreiller**	deckchair	**la chaise**
towel	**la serviette**		**longue**
matches	**les allumettes**	sunshade	**le parasol**
soap	**le savon**	dustbin	**la poubelle**

Animals

horse	**le cheval**	goat	**la chèvre**
rabbit	**le lapin**	sheep	**le mouton**
cow	**la vache**	hen	**la poule**

LANGUAGE NOTES

VOUS ÊTES BIEN MONSIEUR ET MADAME GREEN?

"**Bien**" normally means "fine" or "well", as in these examples:

Bien, Monsieur. (*Fine, Sir.*)
Mon fils parle bien français. (*My son speaks French well.*)

But it can also be used in seeking confirmation of what you think to be so:

Vous êtes bien Madame Green? (*I am right in thinking you are Mrs Green, aren't I?*)

QUELLE BELLE SALLE DE SÉJOUR!

You already know that "**quel**", "**quelle**", "**quels**", "**quelles**" mean "which?" or "what?", as in:

Quelle maison préférez-vous? (*Which house do you prefer?*)

But these words can also introduce an exclamation, "What a . . . !", for instance:

Quelle belle chambre! (*What a beautiful bedroom!*)

BEAU AND BELLE

"**Beau**" means "beautiful". When it is used to describe a feminine noun, it becomes "**belle**":

un beau village (*a beautiful village*)
une belle église (*a beautiful church*)

DONNER AND DONNER SUR

"**Donner**" means "to give". But add the word "**sur**" (*on*), and it becomes the French expression for "to look out onto":

Voulez-vous me donner votre numéro de téléphone? (*Would you give me your telephone number?*)
La chambre donne sur la rue. (*The bedroom looks out onto the street.*)

-ISME, -ION AND -TÉ

The French for some English words is very easy to guess – especially if the English word ends in "ism" or "ion" or "ty". So we don't need to give you the English translations of these:

le communisme	la conversation	l'électricité
l'enthousiasme	l'information	la nécessité
le journalisme	la profession	la possibilité
l'optimisme	la station	la spécialité
le rhumatisme	la vaccination	

Sometimes you might be able to guess the French for an English word by thinking first of an alternative word in English, ending in "ion":

increase **l'augmentation**   entertainment **la distraction**

PROMENADES

"**Faire une promenade**" means "to take a walk", but the word "**promenade**" can be adapted to other forms of moving about:

faire une promenade en voiture (*to go for a car ride*)
faire une promenade en bateau (*to go for a boat trip*)
faire une promenade à bicyclette (*to go for a bicycle ride*)
faire une promenade à cheval (*to go horse-riding*)

 ORDINAL NUMBERS

It is easy to turn a number in French – say, two or three (**deux, trois**) – into its ordinal, "second", "third": just add "**ième**", to make "**deuxième**", "**troisième**".

If the number ends in "e", then leave out the "e" before adding **"ième"**: **quatre – quatrième.**

However, learn these three exceptions:

first **premier**   fifth **cinquième**   ninth **neuvième**

EIGHTY-ONE TO A HUNDRED

81 **quatre-vingt-un**	92 **quatre-vingt-douze**
82 **quatre-vingt-deux**	94 **quatre-vingt-quatorze**
87 **quatre-vingt-sept**	96 **quatre-vingt-seize**
89 **quatre-vingt-neuf**	98 **quatre-vingt-dix-huit**
90 **quatre-vingt-dix**	99 **quatre-vingt-dix-neuf**
91 **quatre-vingt-onze**	100 **cent**

In Belgium and Switzerland the French for 70, 80 and 90 is much simpler than in France. There they say **"septante"**, **"octante"** and **"nonante"**.

ŒUF AND AIL

Notice the pronunciation of these two food words. If you are talking about just one egg, **"l'œuf"** is pronounced "lerf". But if you are talking about more than one egg, the "f" sound disappears – **"les œufs"** is pronounced "lay zer".

You may already have heard the play on words, "Un œuf is enough".

The word for "garlic", **"ail"**, is pronounced "ah'ee". So in dialogue 4, there was a touch of humour when the tourist said **"A l'ail? . . . Aïe, aïe!"**, for **"ail"** and **"aïe"** are pronounced in exactly the same way.

BOUILLABAISSE AND OTHER SOUPS

"Bouillabaisse" is a fish soup as described in dialogue 4. Some other, perhaps less exotic, soups are:

la soupe au chou (*cabbage soup*)
la soupe aux légumes (*vegetable soup*)
la soupe à l'oignon (*onion soup*)
la soupe aux petits pois (*pea soup*)
la soupe aux poireaux (*leek soup*)
la soupe à la tomate (*tomato soup*)

1. QU'EST-CE QUI VOUS INTÉRESSE?

Here's a notice giving details of the coming week's entertainment for your village. Study it carefully and then answer the questions below.

PONTEVES

Programme des activités de la semaine du 20 au 26 août

LUNDI	Cinéma: **Indochine** avec Catherine Deneuve – 20h
MARDI	**Match de football**, Fréjus contre Bournemouth
	Terrain de camping, 15h
MERCREDI	**Discothèque** "Le Rendez-vous" – 22h
JEUDI	**Concours de pétanque** – Place de la Mairie, 14h
VENDREDI	**Barbecue en plein air** – Restaurant "Mon Plaisir", 21h
SAMEDI	Conférence avec projection de diapositives:
	"**Les ruines romaines de la région**" – 17h
DIMANCHE	**Fête du Village**
	Défilé de chars fleuris, fanfare, loterie – 14h
	Feu d'artifice, bal en plein air – 21h30

---

a. Vous aimez le sport. Quelles activités vous intéressent?
b. Vous aimez danser. Quelles activités vous intéressent?
c. Vous aimez la culture. Quels programmes vous intéressent?
d. Vous aimez manger. Quelle soirée vous intéresse?
e. Vous aimez les fêtes. Quel programme vous intéresse?

 ## 2. "LE PARADIS"

Use the tape, if you can, to practise taking part in the following scene, in which you have just arrived at your gîte. You will need this vocabulary:

patio	**la terrasse**	pleasant	**agréable**
swimming pool	**la piscine**	now	**maintenant**
invoice	**la facture**	everything	**tout**
deposit	**la caution**	to use	**utiliser**
wonderful	**magnifique**	to look (at)	**regarder**

Owner: **Bonjour, Madame. Bonjour, Monsieur.**
You: Good afternoon, Monsieur Blanchet.
Owner: **Vous avez fait bon voyage?**
You: Yes. Excellent, thank you.
Owner: **Entrez, entrez. Vous voulez probablement visiter la maison.**
You: The house is beautiful! And two lovely bathrooms!
Owner: **Et maintenant le jardin.**
You: The garden's beautiful too. Can we use the swimming pool?
Owner: **Oui, Madame. Elle est à votre disposition pour toute la semaine.**
You: Look at the patio! What a huge barbecue!
Owner: **Oui. Vous pouvez manger ici le midi et le soir.**
You: Wonderful! Wonderful! Everything's perfect.
Owner: **Très bien.**
You: Is there a deposit to pay?
Owner: **Oui. Voici la facture.**
You: But . . . but . . . that's not the price we . . .
Owner: **Vous êtes bien Monsieur et Madame Smith?**
You: No. We're Mr and Mrs Green! The name of this house <u>is</u> "Le Paradis", 1 rue des Fleurs?
Owner: **Ah non, Madame. Le numéro 1, c'est la maison à côté.**
You: The small white house next door?
Owner: **Oui, Madame. Elle est très agréable aussi.**

FORGET-ME-NOT

French word	English association
l'augmentation (*increase*)	augment
le cheval (*horse*)	cavalry
la mer (*sea*)	maritime

WORD LIST

MASCULINE NOUNS

l'ail	garlic
le bal	dance
le château	castle
le cheval	horse
le fils	son
les fruits	fruit
le jardin	garden
le lac	lake
le marché	market
l'œuf	egg
le siècle	century
le sport	sport
les sports nautiques	water sports
le supermarché	supermarket
le tourisme	tourism
le village	village

FEMININE NOUNS

la bicyclette	bicycle
la caution	deposit
la côte	coast
les courses	shopping
la cuisine	kitchen; cooking
les distractions	entertainment
l'épicerie	grocer's
la facture	invoice
la ferme	farm
la fête	festival
la fille	daughter
la maison	house
la mer	sea
la montagne	mountain
la piscine	swimming pool
la promenade (à pied)	walk
la rue	street
les ruines	ruins
la salle de séjour	living room
la terrasse	patio
la vallée	valley

donner	to give
donner sur	to look out on
entrer	to enter
équiper	to equip
faire les courses	to go shopping
préférer	to prefer
regarder	to look (at)
utiliser	to use

agréable	pleasant
ancien	old
Bienvenue . . . !	Welcome . . . !
local	local
magnifique	wonderful
maintenant	now
parfait	perfect
populaire	popular
tout	everything

10 Money & Shopping

1. LA BANQUE

Tourist: Je voudrais changer des chèques de voyage anglais en francs.
I would like to change some English traveller's cheques into francs.

Bank clerk: Oui, Monsieur. Malheureusement, la livre n'est pas très forte en ce moment.
Yes, Sir. Unfortunately, the pound is not very strong at the moment.

Tourist: Je sais. Quel est le taux de change aujourd'hui?
I know. What is the exchange rate today?

Bank clerk: Huit francs cinquante.
Eight francs fifty.

2. COMBIEN VOULEZ-VOUS CHANGER?

Bank clerk: Combien de livres voulez-vous changer?
How many pounds do you want to change?

Tourist: Cent livres. Je voudrais des petits billets. C'est à dire des billets de cent francs et de cinquante francs.
A hundred pounds. I would like small notes. That is, 100 franc and 50 franc notes.

Bank clerk: Oui, Monsieur. Voilà . . . Cinq cents, six cents, sept cents et huit cents francs. Je vous donne le reste en petite monnaie.
Right, Sir. Here you are . . . Five hundred, six hundred, seven hundred and eight hundred francs. I'll give you the rest in small change.

3. LES CARTES POSTALES

Tourist: J'ai choisi ces trois cartes postales. Ce sont des vues de la région, n'est-ce pas?
I have chosen these three postcards. They are views of this area, aren't they?

Tobacconist: Oui, Monsieur. Ce sont des paysages de la Provence.
Yes, Sir. They are landscapes of Provence.

Tourist: Avez-vous aussi des timbres pour l'Angleterre?
Do you also have stamps for England?

Tobacconist: Oui . . . C'est tout?
Yes . . . Is that all?

Tourist: J'ai pris aussi ce journal anglais.
I've also taken this English newspaper.

Tobacconist: Bien. Ça fait vingt-trois francs en tout.
Right. That makes twenty-three francs altogether.

Note: In France, a tobacconist's is the only place other than the post office where you can buy stamps.

82

4. AU MARCHÉ

Stallholder: Approchez, approchez, Messieurs-Dames . . .
Deux kilos de pêches . . . vingt-cinq francs
seulement. Elles sont parfumées, elles sont
délicieuses. Goûtez, Madame . . .
Roll up, roll up, Ladies and Gentlemen . . . Two kilos
of peaches . . . only twenty-five francs. They smell
good, they taste delicious . . . Have a taste, Madam . . .

Tourist: Oh oui, c'est vrai. Elles sont très juteuses. Trois
livres de pêches mûres, s'il vous plaît.
Oh yes, it's true. They are very juicy. Three pounds
of ripe peaches, please.

Stallholder: Et avec ceci? Du melon de la région? Des
prunes, des olives, des courgettes, du thym de
Provence? De la salade fraîche? Trois francs la
pièce.
Anything else? Locally grown melons? Plums, olives
courgettes, thyme from Provence? Fresh lettuces?
Three francs each.

5. QUELLE VARIÉTÉ!

Tourist: Quelle variété de fruits et de légumes frais! Un
kilo de prunes, s'il vous plaît, un petit melon,
pas trop mûr, une salade et un peu de persil.
What a variety of fresh fruits and vegetables! A kilo
of plums, please, a small melon, not too ripe, a
lettuce and some parsley.

6. LE PAIN

Tourist: Pardon, Monsieur. Pour le pain, c'est où?
Excuse me. Where do we get bread?

Stallholder: A la boulangerie, si vous voulez une baguette,
ou sur le marché, si vous préférez le pain de
campagne.
At the baker's if you want a baguette, or in the
market, if you prefer farmhouse bread.

Tourist: Merci beaucoup. Nous allons acheter les deux . . .
Thank you very much. We are going to buy both . . .

Stallholder: Ah, les Anglais! Ils aiment bien le pain français!
Ah, the English! They love French bread!

INFORMATION

FRENCH BANKS

Opening hours (les heures d'ouverture)
Bank opening hours vary from town to town. Like most French shops, the banks often close at lunchtime, but they remain open all day on "market day" (**le jour du marché**).

French money
Banknotes (**les billets de banque**) are quite attractive, as each represents a different famous person from the past:

500 F Blaise Pascal, 1623-62, writer
200 F Montesquieu, 1689-1755, writer and philosopher
100 F Eugène Delacroix, 1798-1869, painter
50 F   (a new, smaller note than the others) Antoine de Saint-Exupéry, 1900-44, pilot and writer. One of his best-known works is *Le Petit Prince*.
20 F   Claude Debussy, 1862-1918, composer

Coins (**les pièces**) all include the words "**Liberté, Égalité, Fraternité**", the motto of France since the French Revolution, on one side and "**République française**" on the other. The coins are: **10 F** silver with yellow outer ring;
5 F, 2 F, 1 F silver;
50, 20, 10, and **5 centimes** yellow.

Credit cards
You'll have no problem using normal credit cards in France.

SHOPPING

Although supermarkets and hypermarkets are very popular, many French people continue to go to their local baker, butcher and grocer (**le boulanger, le boucher, l'épicier**), preferring the personal and individual service they receive there. You simply must feast your eyes on the window display of any French **pâtisserie**!

In most towns you will find department stores (**les grands magasins**), but you can shop more cheaply at **Monoprix** and **Prisunic** (where, originally, everything was one price), which are similar to Woolworths.

Paris, of course, remains rather special, particularly as regards fashion. Large department stores like **les Galeries Lafayette** and **Au Printemps** cater for all tastes and ages, but some people will always prefer the famous designer labels of a **grand couturier** such as **Yves Saint-Laurent** or **Christian Dior**; they're to be found in rue du Faubourg-St-Honoré and avenue Montaigne.

Finally, an absolute must if you're in Paris is **le Forum des Halles**, rue Pierre-Lescot, with its 200 shops and numerous restaurants.

Bonne journée!

LANGUAGE NOTES

SOME MORE NATIONALITIES

the English	**les Anglais**	the Italians	**les Italiens**
the Belgians	**les Belges**	the Japanese	**les Japonais**
the British	**les Britanniques**	the Russians	**les Russes**
the French	**les Français**	the Spanish	**les Espagnols**
the Germans	**les Allemands**		

MALHEUREUSEMENT

"**Malheureusement**" means "unfortunately". The little word "**mal**" means "badly" and acts as a negative prefix. So "**heureusement**" on its own means "fortunately". Here are some other positives and negatives with "**mal**":

bien (*good*)	**mal** (*badly*)
bonheur (*happiness*)	**malheur** (*unhappiness*)
heureux (*happy*)	**malheureux** (*unhappy*)
honnête (*honest*)	**malhonnête** (*dishonest*)
sain (*healthy*)	**malsain** (*unhealthy*)
traiter (*to treat*)	**maltraiter** (*to mistreat*)

HEUREUX, HEUREUSE

Words ending in "**x**" like "**heureux**" change this "**x**" to "**se**" in the feminine "**heureuse**". Two other examples are "**délicieux**", "**délicieuse**" and "**juteux**", "**juteuse**".

N'EST-CE PAS?

This expression is like the English "isn't it?", "aren't you?", "don't they?" that we tag on to the end of a question. E.g.:

Vos enfants nagent bien, n'est-ce pas? (*Your children swim well, don't they?*)

Vous vendez des timbres, n'est-ce pas? (*You sell stamps, don't you?*)

Ce sont des vues de la région, n'est-ce pas? (*They are views of the region, aren't they?*)

BEAUCOUP AND UN PEU

"**Beaucoup**" means "a lot" and "**un peu**" means "a little". Both take "**de**" in cases like:

beaucoup de fruits (*a lot of fruit*)
un peu de sel (*a little salt*)

PRONOUNCING NUMBERS

On their own, "**cinq**", "**six**" and "**huit**" are pronounced "sang-k", "seess" and "ü'eet". But when they are followed by "**cent**", i.e. 500, 600 and 800, their final letter is silent:

500 sounds like "sang sahng"
600 sounds like "see sahng"
800 sounds like "ü'ee sahng"

The same silencing of the final letter happens when "**cinq**", "**six**", "**huit**" and "**dix**" are followed by "**francs**":

5F sounds like "sang frahng"
10F sounds like "dee frahng"

LE LIVRE AND LA LIVRE

"**La livre**" is "pound". In an earlier chapter we met "**le livre**" (*book*). Normally it doesn't matter very much if you get the gender of a French noun wrong – but you can see that there might be some confusion with "**livre**"! Here are some other words whose meaning changes depending on whether it is "**le**" or "**la**":

le manche (*handle*)	**la Manche** (*the Channel*)
le poste (*job; radio/TV set*)	**la poste** (*post office*)
le somme (*snooze*)	**la somme** (*sum*)
le tour (*walk; tour; turn*)	**la tour** (*tower; high-rise block*)

LETTUCE SALAD

The word "**la salade**" has two meanings, "salad" as a meal or simply "lettuce". (Another word for "lettuce" is "**la laitue**".)

une salade composée (*a mixed salad*)
de la salade fraîche (*fresh lettuce*)

PLUMS AND PRUNES

"**Une prune**" is not what you expect: it is "a plum".
"A prune" is "**un pruneau**".

COUNTRY

"The country" (as opposed to the town) is "**la campagne**". But the word to use for "country" when you mean a "nation", like France, is "**le pays**".

SHOPS

la boucherie (*butcher's*)	**la charcuterie** (*delicatessen*)
la boulangerie (*baker's*)	**la papeterie** (*stationer's*)
l'épicerie (*grocer's*)	**la pharmacie** (*chemist's*)
le grand magasin	**la poissonnerie** (*fishmonger's*)
(*department store*)	**le supermarché** (*supermarket*)

YOUR TURN

1. COULD YOU COPE AT THE BANK?

Take part in this conversation, using the tape if you can. You can check your part with the key on page 104.

You: I'd like to change 200 pounds sterling into French francs. Unfortunately, the pound isn't very strong at the moment.

Clerk: **Non. C'est vrai. Le taux de change aujourd'hui est de 8.50F.**

You:	I'd like small notes, please.
Clerk:	**Malheureusement, j'ai seulement des billets de 200F . . . Attendez! Je vais demander des petits billets à ma collègue.**
You:	It doesn't matter. I'll take what (**ce que**) you have got.

2. AT THE TOBACCONIST'S

Now try buying some postcards. (Notice that "**journal**" becomes "**journaux**" in the plural.)

You:	I've chosen these five postcards with landscapes of Provence. Do you have stamps for England?
Shopkeeper:	**Pour l'Angleterre? Vous êtes Anglais? Vous parlez bien français. J'ai des journaux anglais là-bas, si ça vous intéresse.**
You:	Thank you, but we bought an English newspaper this morning in the hotel. How much does that come to in all?
Shopkeeper:	**Ça fait 35F.**

3. EAVESDROP!

Best of all, if you can, listen to the tape where you will hear snippets from four conversations in different kinds of shop. In each case, say which kind of shop it is. Alternatively, answer the same question by reading the conversations below.

a. **Une baguette et une tarte aux pommes, s'il vous plaît.**
b. **Bonjour, Monsieur. Je voudrais du poisson. Qu'est-ce que vous avez aujourd'hui?**
   J'ai du cabillaud, du thon, du saumon . . .
c. **Avez-vous des timbres pour l'Angleterre?**
   Oui. Pour des cartes postales ou pour des lettres?
d. **Du fromage, s'il vous plaît.**
   Oui, Monsieur. Quel fromage désirez-vous?
   Un camembert.
   Et avec ça?
   Une bouteille de Bordeaux rouge.
   Ah! Vous aimez les bonnes choses!
e. **Cette robe est très jolie.**
   Oui, mais je n'aime pas beaucoup la couleur.
f. **Je ne peux pas vous donner d'antibiotiques pour votre infection sans ordonnance.**

FORGET-ME-NOT

French word	English association
l'épicerie (*grocer's*)	spices
faible (*weak*)	feeble
fort (*strong*)	fortitude
honnête (*honest*)	honest (the circumflex, ^, often becomes "s" in English)
le somme (*snooze*)	somnambulist
vendre (*to sell*)	vending machine

WORD LIST

MASCULINE NOUNS

le bureau de tabac	tobacconist's
le champignon	mushroom
le chèque de voyage	traveller's cheque
le chou	cabbage
le chou-fleur	cauliflower
le melon	melon
le pays	country
le paysage	scenery
le persil	parsley
les petits pois	peas
le pruneau	prune
le raisin	grape
le reste	remainder
le taux de change	exchange rate
le thym	thyme
le timbre	stamp

approcher	to approach
changer	to change
goûter	to taste
nager	to swim
vendre	to sell

délicieux	delicious
faible	weak
fort	strong

FEMININE NOUNS

la banque	bank
la betterave	beetroot
la campagne	country
la carotte	carrot
la carte postale	postcard
la cerise	cherry
la fraise	strawberry
la livre	pound
l'olive	olive
la pêche	peach
la poire	pear
la pomme	apple
la pomme de terre	potato
la poste	post office
la prune	plum
la tomate	tomato
la vue	view

frais (fem. fraîche)	fresh
heureusement	fortunately
juteux	juicy
mal	badly
malheureusement	unfortunately
mauvais	bad
mûr	ripe
vrai	true

11 At the Chemist's

While it's rare to have to call a doctor (**un médecin**) when you're on holiday, it's not unusual to need something from the chemist's, perhaps for a stomach upset (**l'estomac dérangé**), a cold (**un rhume**), a sore throat (**un mal de gorge**), a graze (**une écorchure**), or sunburn (**des coups de soleil**). So imagine yourself going along to the nearest **pharmacie**, and to the dentist.

 1. LES COUPS DE SOLEIL

> *Tourist:* Bonjour, Monsieur. Nous sommes en France depuis une semaine et j'ai attrapé de terribles coups de soleil.
> *Good morning/afternoon. We've been in France for a week and I've got dreadful sunburn.*
>
> *Chemist:* Avez-vous mal à la tête? Avez-vous de la température?
> *Does your head ache? Have you got a temperature?*

Tourist: Non. Je ne pense pas. Mais les coups de soleil
me font très mal.
No. I don't think so. But the sunburn is very painful.
Chemist: Voici une lotion qui va vous soulager.
Appliquez-la régulièrement sur votre corps.
*Here's a lotion which will soothe it. Apply it
regularly over your body.*

2. UNE LOTION, PAS UNE BOISSON!
Tourist: Merci. Un flacon, c'est assez?
Thank you. Is one bottle enough?
Chemist: Oui, Madame. Attention, c'est une lotion, pas
une boisson! Et surtout évitez le soleil. Il est très
chaud ici. Vous avez peut-être besoin d'une
crème protectrice plus forte.
Yes, Madam. Be careful, it's a lotion, not a drink!
And above all, avoid the sun. It's very hot here.
Perhaps you need a stronger protective cream.
Tourist: Oui. Vous avez raison. C'est plus prudent.
Yes. You're right. It's wiser.

3. L'ESTOMAC DÉRANGÉ
Tourist: Et pouvez-vous me donner quelque chose pour
mon mari? Il a l'estomac dérangé.
*And can you give me something for my husband? He
has an upset stomach.*
Chemist: Qu'est-ce qu'il a mangé?
What has he eaten?
Tourist: Hier? Du poisson avec une sauce au vin
délicieuse.
Yesterday? Fish with a delicious wine sauce.
Chemist: Est-ce qu'il a la diarrhée?
Has he got diarrhoea?
Tourist: Oui.
Yes.
Chemist: Voilà. Votre mari doit prendre deux de ces
comprimés par jour. Il doit boire beaucoup
d'eau minérale.
*Here you are. Your husband must take two of these
tablets a day. He must drink lots of mineral water.*

4. CHEZ LE DENTISTE

Tourist: Bonjour, Madame. Je crois que j'ai perdu un morceau de dent. J'ai une douleur vive au fond, à droite . . .
Good morning/afternoon. I think I've lost a piece of tooth. I have a sharp pain at the back, on the right . . .

Dentist: Oui. Vous avez raison. La dent est cassée.
Yes. You're right. The tooth is broken.

Tourist: J'ai mangé un petit pain ce matin avec mon café et il était si dur!
I ate a roll with my coffee this morning and it was so hard!

Dentist: Prenez plutôt un croissant ou une brioche demain . . . De toutes façons, ce n'est pas grave.
You'd better have a croissant or a bun tomorrow . . . Anyway, it's not serious.

5. UN PETIT SOUVENIR DE LA FRANCE

Dentist: Je vais vous plomber la dent mais, franchement, vous avez besoin d'une couronne.
I'm going to fill your tooth, but, frankly, you need a crown.

Tourist: Oui. Je vais aller voir mon dentiste la semaine prochaine en Angleterre . . . Merci. Combien est-ce que je vous dois?
Yes. I'll go and see my dentist next week in England . . . Thank you. How much do I owe you?

Dentist: Rien du tout. Ce sera un petit souvenir de la France. Mon mari est Anglais.
Nothing at all. It will be a little souvenir of France. My husband is English.

INFORMATION

EMERGENCY MEDICAL TREATMENT FOR VISITORS TO FRANCE

As a UK visitor to France, you are entitled to reduced-cost emergency medical treatment, provided that you are in possession of a completed and stamped Form E111, available from post offices before you leave. "Reduced-cost" means that you can receive a refund of about 75% of the standard medical fee paid and between 40% and 70% of the cost of most prescribed medicines. Make sure that the doctor or dentist works within the French NHS system and also that he or she hands you a form (**une feuille de soins**) with details on it of the treatment given. Stick on the stamps (**les vignettes**) from any medicines that you get from the pharmacist, sign the form, date it and take or send it to the local Sickness Insurance Office (**la Caisse Primaire d'Assurance-Maladie**) for a refund.

We must emphasize, however, that Form E111 will NOT cover you for such emergencies as repatriation to the UK, loss of luggage/money/credit cards, compensation for delayed departures, etc. Clearly, for this kind of cover, you need to buy private insurance.

FRENCH DOCTORS AND HOSPITALS

French people don't have to register with a particular doctor as we do in Britain. They can choose any doctor, changing as often as they want. When they go to a surgery, they pay about 120 francs, but a home visit, of course, costs more. When a stay in **un hôpital** or **une clinique privée** becomes necessary, a large part of the cost of the treatment is paid for by **la Sécurité Sociale** and the patient is responsible for the rest, unless s/he has **une mutuelle** (back-up insurance).

LANGUAGE NOTES

DEPUIS

In English we say "We <u>have been</u> in France for one week". In French this is "**Nous sommes en France depuis une semaine**", which translates literally as "We <u>are</u> in France since one week". When you think about it, the French version, which uses the present tense, is the more logical – for, at the time we are speaking, we <u>are</u> still in France! To the French, the English use of the past tense appears odd.

Here are some more examples of "**depuis**" with the present tense:

J'apprends le français depuis deux mois. (*I have been learning French for two months.*)
Depuis quand avez-vous mal à la tête? (*How long* – literally *"since when" – have you had a headache?*)

J'AI MAL À . . .

Hopefully you will not need it, but you had better learn this construction:

J'ai mal au bras. (*My arm hurts.*)
J'ai mal à la cheville. (*My ankle hurts.*)
J'ai mal aux dents. (*I have toothache.*)
J'ai mal à l'oreille. (*My ear hurts.*)
J'ai mal au(x) pied(s). (*My foot/feet hurt/s.*)
J'ai mal à la tête. (*My head aches.*)
J'ai mal au ventre. (*My stomach hurts.*)

TO NEED (AVOIR BESOIN DE)

"**Avoir besoin de**" means literally "to have need of". E.g.:

J'ai besoin d'un lit supplémentaire. (*I need an extra bed.*)
J'ai besoin d'envoyer un fax. (*I need to send a fax.*)
Il a besoin d'un oreiller. (*He needs a pillow.*)
Nous avons besoin de savon. (*We need soap.*)
Vous avez besoin de serviettes. (*You need towels.*)
Elles ont besoin de fixer un rendez-vous. (*They need to arrange a meeting.*)

AVOIR RAISON (TO BE RIGHT)

In several cases, like this, French uses "**avoir**" (*to have*) where English uses "to be". The French for "You are right" is "**Vous avez raison**." "You are wrong" is "**Vous avez tort**."
Some other expressions with "**avoir**" are:

to be hungry	**avoir faim** (e.g. **J'ai faim**.)	
to be thirsty	**avoir soif** (e.g. **Il a soif**.)	
to be cold	**avoir froid** (e.g. **Nous avons froid**.)	
to be warm	**avoir chaud** (e.g. **Avez-vous chaud?**)	

IT'S WARM – AND OTHER WEATHER TERMS

To say "It's warm" about the weather, you need the verb "**faire**" (*to do, to make*). For instance:

Il fait chaud. (*It's warm.*)   **Il fait du vent**. (*It's windy.*)
Il fait froid. (*It's cold.*)

Rain and snow have their own verbs:

Il pleut. (*It's raining.*)   **Il neige**. (*It's snowing.*)

BOIRE (TO DRINK)

This verb has an irregular pattern:

Je bois un café-crème. (*I'm drinking a white coffee.*)
Il/Elle boit un thé au citron. (*He/She's drinking a lemon tea.*)
Nous buvons un Orangina. (*We're drinking an Orangina.*)
Vous buvez du vin. (*You're drinking wine.*)
Ils/Elles boivent de la bière. (*They're drinking beer.*)

DEVOIR (TO HAVE TO AND TO OWE)

Remember the expression "**Il faut réserver une table**", meaning "I/You/He/She/We/They must reserve a table"? (See page 48). If you want to be more specific, you can use "**devoir**", which means "to have to". It has an irregular pattern:

Je dois attraper le train. (*I must catch the train.*)
Il doit appliquer la lotion. (*He must apply the lotion.*)
Elle doit acheter des lunettes de soleil. (*She must buy some sunglasses.*)
Nous devons apprendre l'allemand. (*We must learn German.*)
Vous devez aller à la pharmacie. (*You must go to the chemist's.*)
Ils doivent éviter le soleil. (*They must avoid the sun.*)
Elles doivent boire de l'eau. (*They must drink water.*)

The verb "**devoir**" also has another meaning, "to owe", as in:

Combien est-ce que je vous dois? (*How much do I owe you?*)

BOTTLES

The usual word for "bottle" is "**la bouteille**". "**Un flacon**" is a smaller bottle, as used for medicine or perfume, for example.

ATTRAPER (TO CATCH)

"**Attraper**" is used for catching a bus or train (**attraper un bus/ un train**), for catching a cold (**attraper un rhume**), and for getting sunburn (**attraper des coups de soleil**).

POISONOUS PRONUNCIATION

Be careful, when you are talking about fish, to pronounce "**le poisson**" correctly – "pwah-song". If you were to say "pwah-zong", you would be understood as talking about "poison" ("**le poison**").

THINGS YOU MIGHT NEED AT THE CHEMIST'S

cough sweets	**des pastilles pour la toux**
throat sweets	**des pastilles pour la gorge**
eye drops	**des gouttes pour les yeux**
ear drops	**des gouttes pour les oreilles**
first-aid plasters	**des pansements adhésifs**
mild laxative	**un laxatif léger**
anti-mosquito cream	**une crème anti-moustiques**

JE PENSE QUE/JE CROIS QUE

Either of these expressions can be used for "I think that . . . ".

UN PETIT PAIN

"**Le pain**" is bread. "**Un pain**" is "a loaf". And "**un petit pain**" is "a bread roll". "**Une brioche**" is "a bun".

IL ÉTAIT SI DUR! – TALKING ABOUT THE PAST

The tourist said the bread roll "was so hard": "**Il était si dur!**" "**Était**" is one form of the past of "**être**" (*to be*). It is used to describe how things were in the past. It goes like this:

J'étais en Italie. (*I was in Italy.*)
Il/Elle était malade. (*He/She was ill.*)
Nous étions à la maison. (*We were at home.*)
Vous étiez au chômage. (*You were unemployed.*)
Ils/Elles étaient en colère. (*They were angry.*)

If you go on to learn more French, when you have finished this course, you will learn more about this tense (called the imperfect). This is the form "**avoir**" takes in this past tense:

J'avais un emploi l'année dernière. (*I had a job last year*.)
Il/Elle avait . . . (*He/She had . . .*)
Nous avions . . . (*We had . . .*)
Vous aviez . . . (*You had . . .*)
Ils/Elles avaient . . . (*They had . . .*)

TALKING ABOUT THE FUTURE

Again, if you continue studying French beyond this course, you will learn more about the future forms of verbs. But it will be useful for you now to learn the future forms of "**être**" and "**avoir**". This is how they go:

Je serai à l'hôtel demain. (*I will be at the hotel tomorrow*.)
Il/Elle sera . . . (*He/She will be . . .*)
Nous serons . . . (*We will be . . .*)
Vous serez . . . (*You will be . . .*)
Ils/Elles seront . . . (*They will be . . .*)

J'aurai une autre chambre demain. (*I will have another room tomorrow*.)
Il/Elle aura . . . (*He/She will have . . .*)
Nous aurons . . . (*We will have . . .*)
Vous aurez . . . (*You will have . . .*)
Ils/Elles auront . . . (*They will have . . .*)

LAST AND NEXT

Since you know how to talk of the past and the future, you will find these words useful: "**dernier**" (*last*) and "**prochain**" (*next*):

la semaine dernière (*last week*)
le mois dernier (*last month*)
l'année dernière (*last year*)
la semaine prochaine (*next week*)
le mois prochain (*next month*)
l'année prochaine (*next year*)

YOUR TURN

1. WHAT'S YOUR COMPLAINT?

What ailments would you expect in these circumstances?

a. **Vos chaussures sont trop petites.**

b. **Vous avez trop joué au tennis.**

c. **Vous avez mangé trop de chocolats.**

d. **Vous êtes resté trop longtemps au soleil.**

e. **Vous avez oublié vos lunettes de soleil.**

f. **Vous avez passé la soirée à la discothèque; la musique était insupportable.**

g. **Vous n'êtes pas allé chez le dentiste depuis longtemps.**

h. **Vous avez chanté toute la journée.**

 ## 2. USING YOUR FIRST-AID KIT

Imagine you're with six French friends, each with something wrong. Fortunately, you have your first-aid kit with you. If you can, practise speaking your part with the tape.

Friend 1: **J'ai mal à la tête.**
You: Swallow these tablets with some water.
Friend 2: **J'ai mal aux yeux.**
You: Here are some eye drops.
Friend 3: **J'ai mal à la gorge.**
You: Take these lozenges.
Friend 4: **J'ai attrapé des coups de soleil.**
You: Apply this lotion to your arms and legs.
Friend 5: **J'ai une égratignure au bras.**
You: I've some plasters.
Friend 6: **Je suis constipé.**
You: Take this mild laxative.

3. WHAT'S THE WEATHER LIKE?

Judging by the following clues, describe the weather:

a. **Attention à votre chapeau!**

b. **Prenez un parapluie!**

c. **Ouvrez toutes les fenêtres!**

d. **Les arbres sont tout blancs. Quel beau paysage de Noël!**

e. **Vous avez le nez et les oreilles rouges!**

4. COULD YOU COPE AT THE CHEMIST'S?

Take part in this scene, using the tape if you can. You can check your part with the key on page 105.

You: I'd like a tube of toothpaste, please.

Chemist: **Oui. Quelle marque?**

You: It doesn't matter.

Chemist: **Voilà, Monsieur. Quinze francs.**

You: Thank you. Can you have my photos developed by tomorrow?

Chemist: **Mais, Monsieur, c'est une pharmacie ici. Vous n'êtes pas chez un photographe.**

You: Oh. I'm sorry! It's different in England.

Chemist: **Autres pays, autres mœurs!**

FORGET-ME-NOT

French word	English association
apprendre (*to learn*)	apprentice
attraper (*to catch*)	trap
boire (*to drink*)	beverage
la couverture (*blanket*)	cover
la dent (*tooth*)	dental
envoyer (*to send*)	envoy
éviter (*to avoid*)	inevitable
la faim (*hunger*)	famine
malade (*ill*)	malady
l'oreille (*ear*)	aural
penser (*to think*)	pensive
le soleil (*sun*)	solar
le vent (*wind*)	ventilation

WORD LIST

MASCULINE NOUNS

l'autobus	bus
l'avion	aeroplane
le bras	arm
le chômage	unemployment
le comprimé	tablet
le corps	body
l'emploi	job
l'estomac	stomach
le flacon	small bottle
le laxatif	laxative
le lit	bed
le mari	husband
le médecin	doctor
le morceau	piece, bit
l'oreiller	pillow
le pansement	plaster
le petit pain	bread roll
le rendez-vous	appointment, meeting
le rhume	cold
le savon	soap
le soleil	sun
le souvenir	souvenir; memory
le vent	wind
le ventre	stomach

FEMININE NOUNS

la brioche	bun
la cheville	ankle
la couronne	crown
la couverture	blanket
la dent	tooth
la diarrhée	diarrhoea
la douleur	pain
l'eau minérale	mineral water
l'écorchure	graze
la faim	hunger
la gorge	throat
la goutte	drop
la jambe	leg
la lotion	lotion
les lunettes (de soleil)	(sun)glasses
la neige	snow
l'oreille	ear
la pastille	lozenge, sweet
la semaine	week
la serviette	towel
la température	temperature

appliquer	to apply
apprendre	to learn
avoir faim	to be hungry
avoir raison	to be right
avoir soif	to be thirsty
avoir tort	to be wrong
boire	to drink
casser	to break
déranger	to upset, disturb
envoyer	to send
éviter	to avoid
fixer	to arrange
neiger	to snow
penser	to think
perdre	to lose
pleuvoir	to rain
plomber	to fill (tooth)
soulager	to relieve, soothe

à la maison	at home
au fond	at the back
chaud	warm
dernier	last
dur	hard
en colère	angry
franchement	frankly
froid	cold
léger	light
malade	ill
plutôt	rather
prochain	next
prudent	wise
régulièrement	regularly
supplémentaire	extra
temporairement	temporarily
vif (fem. vive)	acute

Key to "Your Turn"

CHAPTER 2 CHECKING IN

1. What would you say in French?

a. Voici ma carte d'embarquement.
b. Fumeurs, s'il vous plaît.
c. Merci.
d. Non. Quatre valises.
e. Bonjour, Madame.
f. Vérifiez, Monsieur (or Madame).
g. Je garde le petit sac.
h. Ah, voici mon parapluie.
i. i) Avez-vous votre valise?
   ii) Avez-vous votre passeport?
   iii) Avez-vous votre chat?

2. What price?

a. 10 francs; b. 4 francs;
c. 3 francs; d. 9 francs;
e. 100 francs.

CHAPTER 3 DESTINATION PARIS

1. Could you cope?
a. Excusez-moi, Madame.
b. Would you sign this form (or card), please?
c. Quelle table, s'il vous plaît?
d. Du jus d'orange et du café au lait.
e. Pourriez-vous m'apporter du lait, s'il vous plaît?
f. It's straight on.
g. Je suis Écossaise.
h. Tout droit et tournez à droite.

2. On the plane
You: Où est la place numéro 7, s'il vous plaît?
Stewardess: À gauche, Monsieur.
You: Merci . . . Excusez-moi (or: Pardon), Madame . . . c'est ma place. Voici ma carte d'embarquement . . . place numéro 7.
Stewardess: Désirez-vous un journal français, Monsieur?
You: Non, merci. Pourriez-vous m'apporter un verre d'eau?
Stewardess: Voulez-vous mettre le parapluie sous votre siège, s'il vous plaît?
You: Excusez-moi, mais il est trop grand!

CHAPTER 4 AT THE HOTEL

1. Could you cope?
a. Je voudrais une chambre pour une personne.
b. Avec salle de bains, s'il vous plaît.
c. Le petit déjeuner est en supplément?
d. i) La radio ne marche pas.
   ii) Les toilettes ne marchent pas ("Toilet" in French is plural).
   iii) L'ascenseur est en panne.
   iv) Le lit est trop petit.
e. Non, je ne mange pas à l'hôtel ce soir, mais peut-être demain.
f. Mademoiselle, le café est froid.

g. Est-ce que vous acceptez les cartes de crédit?

h. Bonjour. Je voudrais réserver une table pour deux personnes pour midi.

i. i) Nous acceptons les cartes de crédit.
ii) Hôtel trois étoiles.
iii) Nous parlons anglais.
iv) Les chiens et les chats ne sont pas admis.

 2. *Numbers*
Douze; neuf; quinze; quatre; onze; treize; quatorze; sept; deux; cinq.

CHAPTER 5 IN THE RESTAURANT

1. *Could you cope?*

a. Nous avons réservé une chambre dans un petit hôtel.
Nous avons parlé français.
Nous avons loué une voiture.
Nous avons mangé dans un bon restaurant.
Nous avons téléphoné à notre fille en Angleterre.

b. Bonsoir! Nous avons réservé une table pour deux personnes, pour huit heures et demie.

c. Oh yes, you're the English customers who telephoned this morning.

d. Would you like to come this way, please?

e. Pourrions-nous avoir une table près de la fenêtre, s'il vous plaît?

f. Nous avons choisi le menu à 120 francs.

g. A quarter to eight.

h. A quelle heure servez-vous le petit déjeuner?

i. i) la viande; ii) le bifteck; iii) le canard; iv) le poisson; v) le saumon; vi) la truite; vii) la glace; viii) la pâtisserie; ix) le vin; x) le porto.

j. i) À sept heures; ii) À onze heures et quart; iii) À neuf heures et demie.

CHAPTER 6 TOURIST INFORMATION

 1. *Where's the tourist information office?*
Pardon, Madame. Où est le syndicat d'initiative, s'il vous plaît?

 2. *Could you cope in the tourist office?*
You: Bonjour, Madame (or: Monsieur/Mademoiselle). Avez-vous un plan de Paris?
Clerk: Oui, Monsieur. Voilà.
You: Merci. Où est-ce que je peux louer une voiture? Quand pouvons-nous visiter Versailles? Quelles excursions recommandez-vous (or: est-ce que vous recommandez)? Comment pouvons-nous aller à la tour Eiffel? Où est-ce que je peux téléphoner? . . .
Clerk: Je vous recommande aussi de descendre la Seine en bateau-mouche.

 3. *Back at the hotel*
You: Pardon. Où est-ce que je peux acheter des timbres?
Receptionist: Il faut aller à la poste, Madame, ou dans un bureau de tabac . . . Vous êtes Madame Green, non?
You: Oui, c'est ça.
Receptionist: Nous avons reçu ce matin un fax de votre secrétaire.
You: Un fax? De ma secrétaire?
Receptionist: Oui. Un instant . . . Voilà le fax.
You: Merci beaucoup. Mon Dieu . . . j'ai oublié de la payer!

 4. *Fast numbers*
Vingt-neuf; dix-neuf; neuf; trente; vingt et un; vingt-six; quatorze; sept; onze.

CHAPTER 7 A LOST BAG

1. Could you cope?
a. i) Mon parapluie a disparu/a été volé.
ii) La nouvelle robe de ma femme a disparu/a été volée.
iii) Ma serviette a disparu/a été volée.
iv) Ma montre a disparu/a été volée.
b. Mon appareil-photo a disparu de ma chambre.
c. Nous sommes arrivés en France il y a une semaine.
d. i) le trois janvier; ii) le vingt-quatre février; iii) le trente et un août; iv) le seize novembre.
e. Dix-neuf, quarante-quatre, vingt-cinq, trente-trois, zéro un.
f. See list of professions, page 58.
g. It doesn't matter (literally, It's not serious.)
h. Elle est rouge, elle est grande, dedans il y a des chemises, des robes, des livres, des chaussures et un vanity-case bleu.
i. iii: How long are you going to stay in France?

2. At the lost property office
You: Pouvez-vous m'aider? J'ai oublié un sac dans le métro.
Official: Quel jour et à quelle heure, Madame?
You: Hier, vendredi. À trois heures et demie.
Official: Entre quelles stations?
You: Entre Concorde et Opéra.
Official: Pouvez-vous décrire le sac?
You: Il est assez grand, il est blanc et il y a une image de la tour Eiffel sur le côté.
Official: Qu'est-ce qu'il y a dedans?
You: Une belle robe de chambre; je l'ai achetée pour mon mari.

Official: Cette robe de chambre, elle est jaune, rouge, verte et rose?
You: Oui, c'est ça! Avez-vous trouvé la robe de chambre?
Official: Oui. La voici.
You: Oh, merci beaucoup! Elle est belle, non (or: n'est-ce pas)?
Official: Euh . . . oui . . . euh . . . C'est une question de goût.

CHAPTER 8 TRAVELLING BY CAR

1. Could you cope?
a. Bonjour, Monsieur. (Faites) le plein, s'il vous plaît.
b. Super.
c. Voulez-vous vérifier l'eau, s'il vous plaît?
d. Attention au radiateur - il est très chaud!
e. Il faut payer à la caisse?
f. Il pleut à verse. La pluie arrive probablement d'Espagne.
g. Excusez-moi, mais je n'ai pas de monnaie.
h. J'ai seulement un billet de deux cents francs.

2. A routine check
Officer: Bonjour, Madame . . . Monsieur. Vous avez vos papiers, s'il vous plaît?
You: Excusez-moi. Je ne comprends pas.
Officer: Votre permis de conduire, votre assurance, votre carte grise, s'il vous plaît.
You: Oh, maintenant je comprends. Oui, bien sûr, excusez-moi. Voilà, monsieur l'agent.
Officer: Mais où est la photo?
You: Nous n'avons pas de photos en Angleterre.
Officer: C'est votre voiture?
You: Non. Nous avons loué la voiture ce matin.

Officer: Où allez-vous?

You: Nous allons à Lyon.

Officer: D'où venez-vous?

You: De Paris.

Officer: C'est parfait. C'est simplement un contrôle de routine. Bonne route!

You: Oh là là! Je l'ai échappé belle avec ma ceinture!

CHAPTER 9 ARRIVING AT YOUR GÎTE

1. Qu'est-ce qui vous intéresse?

a. Le match de football, Fréjus contre Bournemouth, mardi à 15h, au (sur le) terrain de camping; et le concours de pétanque, jeudi à 14h, Place de la Mairie.

b. La discothèque "Le Rendez-vous", mercredi à 22h; et le bal en plein air, dimanche à 21h30.

c. Le cinéma: le film **Indochine** avec Catherine Deneuve, lundi à 20h; et la conférence avec projection de diapositives sur les ruines romaines de la région, samedi à 17h.

d. Le barbecue en plein air au restaurant "Mon Plaisir", vendredi à 21h.

e. La fête du village avec le défilé de chars fleuris, la fanfare, la loterie, dimanche à 14h, le feu d'artifice et le bal en plein air à 21h30.

2. "Le Paradis"

Owner: Bonjour, Madame. Bonjour, Monsieur.

You: Bonjour, Monsieur Blanchet.

Owner: Vous avez fait bon voyage?

You: Oui, excellent, merci.

Owner: Entrez, entrez. Vous voulez probablement visiter la maison.

You: La maison est belle! Avec deux jolies salles de bains!

Owner: Et maintenant le jardin.

You: Le jardin est beau aussi. Est-ce que nous pouvons utiliser la piscine?

Owner: Oui, Madame. Elle est à votre disposition pour toute la semaine.

You: Regardez* la terrasse! Quel énorme barbecue!

Owner: Oui. Vous pouvez manger ici le midi et le soir.

You: Magnifique! Magnifique! Tout est parfait.

Owner: Très bien.

You: Est-ce qu'il y a une caution à payer?

Owner: Oui. Voici la facture.

You: Mais . . . mais . . . ce n'est pas le prix que nous . . .

Owner: Vous êtes bien Monsieur et Madame Smith?

You: Non. Nous sommes M. et Mme Green! Le nom de cette maison est bien "Le Paradis", 1 rue des Fleurs?

Owner: Ah, non, Madame. Le numéro 1, c'est la maison à côté.

You: La petite maison blanche à côté?

Owner: Oui, Madame. Elle est très agréable aussi.

* Note: If Mrs Green were speaking only to her husband, she would say "**Regarde**" rather than "**Regardez**", and she would call him "**tu**" rather than "**vous**". In this course we have deliberately not included material on the familiar form of "you", "**tu**". You will never be wrong in using "**vous**" to the people you meet as you travel around France.

CHAPTER 10 MONEY AND SHOPPING

1. Could you cope at the bank?

You: Je voudrais changer deux cents livres sterling en francs français. Malheureusement, la livre n'est pas très forte en ce moment.

Clerk: Non. C'est vrai. Le taux de change aujourd'hui est de 8.50F.

You: Je voudrais des petits billets, s'il vous plaît.

Clerk: Malheureusement, j'ai seulement des billets de 200F . . . Attendez! Je vais demander des petits billets à ma collègue.

You: Ça ne fait rien. Je vais prendre ce que vous avez.

 2. At the tobacconist's
You: J'ai choisi ces cinq cartes postales avec les paysages de la Provence. Avez-vous des timbres pour l'Angleterre?

Shopkeeper: Pour l'Angleterre? Vous êtes Anglais? Vous parlez bien français. J'ai des journaux anglais là-bas, si ça vous intéresse.

You: Merci, mais nous avons acheté un journal anglais ce matin à l'hôtel. Ça fait combien en tout?

Shopkeeper: Ça fait 35 francs.

 3. Eavesdrop
a. à la boulangerie; b. à la poissonnerie; c. au bureau de tabac; d. à l'épicerie; e. dans un grand magasin; f. à la pharmacie.

CHAPTER 11 AT THE CHEMIST'S

1. What's your complaint?
a. J'ai mal aux pieds.
b. J'ai mal au bras.
c. J'ai mal au ventre.
d. J'ai attrapé des coups de soleil.
e. J'ai mal aux yeux.
f. J'ai mal aux oreilles.
g. J'ai mal aux dents.
h. J'ai mal à la gorge.

 2. Using your first-aid kit
Friend 1: J'ai mal à la tête.
You: Avalez ces comprimés avec de l'eau.

Friend 2: J'ai mal aux yeux.
You: Voici des gouttes pour les yeux.

Friend 3: J'ai mal à la gorge.
You: Prenez ces pastilles.

Friend 4: J'ai attrapé des coups de soleil.
You: Appliquez cette lotion sur vos bras et sur vos jambes.

Friend 5: J'ai une égratignure au bras.
You: J'ai des pansements.

Friend 6: Je suis constipé.
You: Prenez ce laxatif léger.

3. What's the weather like?
a. Il fait du vent.
b. Il pleut.
c. Il fait chaud.
d. Il neige.
e. Il fait froid.

 4. Could you cope at the chemist's?
You: Je voudrais un tube de dentifrice, s'il vous plaît.

Chemist: Oui. Quelle marque?
You: Ça n'a pas d'importance.

Chemist: Voilà, Monsieur. Quinze francs.

You: Merci. Pouvez-vous faire développer mes photos pour demain?

Chemist: Mais, Monsieur, c'est une pharmacie ici. Vous n'êtes pas chez un photographe.

You: Oh, pardon! C'est différent en Angleterre.

Chemist: Autres pays, autres mœurs!

Mini-Dictionary

A
à at, to
abord
  d'a. first of all
accepter to accept
accord (m.) agreement
  D'a. OK
acheter to buy
à côté de next to
addition (f.) bill
admis admitted, allowed
adresse (f.) address
aéroglisseur (m.) hovercraft
aéroport (m.) airport
affaires (f.pl.) business
  pour a. on business
affectueux affectionate
affreux dreadful
agent (m.) de police police officer
  monsieur l'agent Officer (addressing him)
agrandir to enlarge
agréable pleasant
aider to help
ail (m.) garlic
aimer to like, love
Allemagne (f.) Germany
allemand German
aller to go
  je vais I go
  vous allez you go
  je suis allé(e) I went
  Comment allez-vous? How are you?

allumette (f.) match
ambulance (f.) ambulance
américain American
an (m.) year
ancien, ancienne (f.) old
anglais English
Angleterre (f.) England
année (f.) year
anniversaire (m.) birthday
appareil-photo (m.) camera
appeler to call
  je m'appelle I am called, My name is
appliquer to apply
apporter to bring
apprendre to learn
  j'apprends I learn
  vous apprenez you learn
  j'ai appris I learned
après-midi (m. or f.) afternoon
arbre (m.) tree
argent (m.) money
arriver to arrive
ascenseur (m.) lift
assez fairly, quite; enough
assurance (f.) insurance
attacher to attach, fasten
attendre to wait (for)
  j'attends I wait
  vous attendez you wait
  j'ai attendu I waited
Attention! Be careful!
attraper to catch
aujourd'hui today

106

Au revoir! Goodbye!
aussi also
autobus (m.) bus
autocar (m.) coach
autre other
    autres pays, autres mœurs different countries, different customs
avaler to swallow
avec with
avion (m.) aeroplane
avoir to have
    j'ai I have
    vous avez you have
    j'avais I had
    j'aurai I will have

B
bagages (m.pl.) luggage
baguette (f.) stick of French bread
bal (m.) dance
banque (f.) bank
barbecue (m.) barbecue
bateau (m.) boat
    bateau-mouche cruise boat
beau, belle (f.) beautiful
beaucoup a lot, a great deal
besoin (m.) need
    avoir besoin de to need
betterave (f.) beetroot
bibliothécaire librarian
bibliothèque (f.) library
bicyclette (f.) bicycle
bien well, fine
    bien sûr of course
Bienvenue . . . ! Welcome . . . !
bienvenu welcome
    vous êtes les bienvenus you are welcome
bifteck (m.) steak
billet (m.) ticket; (bank)note
blanc, blanche (f.) white
bleu blue
boire to drink
    je bois I drink
    vous buvez you drink
    j'ai bu I drank
boisson (f.) drink

boîte (f.) box, tin
bon, bonne (f.) good
Bonjour! Good morning!, Good afternoon!
bon marché cheap
Bonsoir! Good evening!
boucherie (f.) butcher's
boulanger (m.) baker
boulangerie (f.) baker's
bouteille (f.) bottle
brioche (f.) bun
brouillard (m.) fog
bureau (m.) office
    b. de tabac tobacconist's
    b. des objets trouvés lost property office

C
ça that
    c'est ça that's right
cabillaud (m.) (fresh) cod
café (m.) coffee
    café au lait coffee with milk
    café-crème white coffee
caisse (f.) cashdesk
canard (m.) duck
car (m.) coach
carte (f.) card; menu; map
    c. de crédit credit card
    c. d'embarquement boarding pass
    c. grise (car) registration document
    c. postale postcard
    c. routière road map
cas (m.) case
casser to break
cathédrale (f.) cathedral
caution (f.) deposit
ce, cette, ces this, these
    ce matin this morning
    ce soir this evening
ceci this
    et avec c.? anything else?
ceinture (f.) belt
célibataire (m. and f.) single person
cerise (f.) cherry
certainement certainly
c'est this is, it is

chambre (f.) (bed)room
champignon (m.) mushroom
chance (f.) luck
changer to change
chanter to sing
chapeau (m.) hat
char (m.) float
chat (m.) cat
chaud warm
  avoir c. to be warm
  il fait c. it's warm
chaussure (f.) shoe
chemise (f.) shirt
chèque (m.) cheque
  c. de voyage traveller's cheque
cher dear, expensive
chercher to look for
cheval (m.) horse
cheville (f.) ankle
chez at the house of
  c. le photographe at the
    photographer's
chien (m.) dog
choisir to choose
chômage (m.) unemployment
chose (f.) thing
chou (m.) cabbage
chou-fleur (m.) cauliflower
chute (f.) de neige snowfall
cinéma (m.) cinema
clé (f.) key
client (m.), cliente (f.) customer
colère (f.) anger
  en c. angry
collègue (m. and f.) colleague
combien? how much?
  combien de temps? how long?
comme like
  comme ça like that
commencer to begin
comment how
  Comment allez-vous? How are you?
commissariat (m.) de police police
  station
comprendre to understand
  je comprends I understand
  vous comprenez you understand

j'ai compris I understood
comprimé (m.) tablet
compris included
  Le petit déjeuner est compris? Is
    breakfast included?
concours (m.) competition
conférence (f.) lecture
connaître to know (person, place)
  je connais I know
  vous connaissez you know
constipé constipated
contacter to contact
content pleased
contenu (m.) contents
contre against
contrôle (m.) de routine routine check
corps (m.) body
côte (f.) coast
côté (m.) side
couleur (f.) colour
coup(s) (m.) de soleil sunburn
courses (f.pl.) shopping
  faire ses courses to do one's
    shopping
court short
couverture (f.) blanket
crème (f.) cream
  c. anti-moustiques anti-mosquito
    cream
croire to believe, think
  je crois I believe
  vous croyez you believe
crudités raw vegetables
cuisine (f.) kitchen; cooking

D
dame (f.) lady
dangereux, -euse (f.) dangerous
dans in
danser to dance
de from, of
décrire to describe
dedans inside
défilé (m.) procession
déjeuner (m.) lunch
  le petit d. breakfast
délicieux, -euse (f.) delicious

demain tomorrow
demander to ask (for)
dent (f.) tooth
dentiste (m. and f.) dentist
depuis since
derrière behind
descendre to go down
désirer to want, wish
dessert (m.) dessert
devant in front of
développer to develop
  faire d. to have developed
devoir to have to; to owe
diapositive (f.) slide (photographic)
diarrhée (f.) diarrhoea
dieu (m.) god
  Mon Dieu! Good heavens!
différent different
dimanche (m.) Sunday
disparaître to disappear
  il a disparu it/he disappeared
disposition (f.) disposal
  à votre d. at your disposal
distractions (f.pl.) entertainment
divorcé divorced
donc so, therefore
donner to give
  donner sur to look out on
douche (f.) shower
douleur (f.) pain
droite (f.) right side
  à d. on the right
du, de la, de l', des some
dur hard

E
eau (f.) water
  e. minérale mineral water
l'échapper belle to have a narrow
  escape
écorchure (f.) graze
écossais Scottish
écrire to write
  j'écris I write
  vous écrivez you write
  j'ai écrit I wrote
église (f.) church

égratignure (f.) scratch
Eh bien . . . Well . . .
en in
  en face de opposite
énorme enormous
ensuite afterwards
entre between
entrer to enter, come in, go in
  je suis entré(e) I went in
environ about, around
envoyer to send
épicerie (f.) grocer's
équiper to equip
erreur (f.) mistake
Espagne (f.) Spain
espagnol Spanish
essence (f.) petrol
est-ce que literally, "Is it that . . . ?"
  (introduces a question)
estomac (m.) stomach
  l'e. dérangé upset stomach
et and
été (m.) summer
été been
  il a été he/it has been
étoile (f.) star
être to be
  je suis I am
  vous êtes you are
  j'étais I was
  je serai I will be
éviter to avoid
exceptionnellement as an exception
excursion (f.) excursion
Excusez-moi! Excuse me!, I'm sorry!
exiger to demand
extrêmement extremely

F
face
  en f. de opposite
facture (f.) invoice
faim (f.) hunger
  avoir f. to be hungry
faire to do, make, have (something
  done)
  Ça ne fait rien It doesn't matter

Ça fait combien? How much does it come to?

faut
Il faut . . . I/You/He/She/We/They must . . .

femme (f.) woman; wife
fenêtre (f.) window
ferme (f.) farm
fête (f.) festival, fête
feu (m.) d'artifice fireworks
fiche (f.) card, form
fille (f.) daughter
film (m.) film
fils (m.) son
fixer to arrange
f. un rendez-vous to fix an appointment
flacon (m.) (small) bottle
fleur (f.) flower
fleuri decorated with flowers
fond
au f. at the back
forfait(m.)-skieur ski pass
fort strong
frais, fraîche (f.) fresh
fraise (f.) strawberry
français French
franchement frankly
froid cold
avoir f. to be cold
il fait f. it's cold
fromage (m.) cheese
fruits (m.pl.) fruit
fumeurs smoking
non-f. non-smoking

G
gallois Welsh
garder to keep
gare (f.) station
gauche (f.) left side
à g. on the left
gendarme (m.) country policeman
généralement generally
gîte (m.) self-catering cottage (flat)
glace (f.) ice cream; ice
gorge (f.) throat
goût (m.) taste

goûter to taste
gouttes (f.pl.) drops
g. pour les oreilles ear drops
g. pour les yeux eye drops
grand large
gratuit free
grave serious
griller to grill
gris grey
guide (m.) guide

H
habiter to live
heure (f.) hour
à quelle h.? at what time?
Quelle heure est-il? What time is it?
heureusement fortunately
hier yesterday
hiver (m.) winter
hôtel (m.) hotel
huile (f.) oil

I
ici here
par ici this way
il he, it
il y a there is, there are; ago
image (f.) picture
immédiatement immediately
important important
Indochine (f.) Indochina
ingénieur (m.) engineer
instant (m.) moment
Un i.,s'il vous plaît One moment, please
insupportable unbearable
intéressant interesting
intéresser to interest
inviter to invite
irlandais Irish
italien, -ienne (f.) Italian

J
jambe (f.) leg
japonais Japanese
jardin (m.) garden
jaune yellow

je I
jeudi Thursday
joli pretty
jouer to play
jour (m.) day
journal (m.), -aux (pl.) newspaper
journaliste (m. and f.) journalist
journée (f.) day
jus (m.) d'orange orange juice
juste just
juteux, -euse (f.) juicy

L
là-bas over there
lac (m.) lake
lait (m.) milk
laxatif (m.) laxative
  l. léger mild laxative
le, la, les the
  le him, it
  la her, it
  les them
leçon (f.) lesson
leçons de ski skiing lessons
léger light
légume (m.) vegetable
lent slow
lentement slowly
lettre (f.) letter
librairie (f.) bookshop
libre free
lit (m.) bed
livre (m.) book
livre (f.) (sterling) pound (sterling)
loin far
Londres London
long, -ue (f.) long
longtemps a long time
lotion (f.) lotion
louer to hire
lundi Monday
lunettes (f.pl.) (de soleil) (sun)glasses

M
magasin (m.) shop
magnifique wonderful
maintenant now
mairie (f.) town hall

mais but
maison (f.) house
  à la m. at home
mal badly
mal (m.) ache
  j'ai mal à . . . my . . . hurts
malade ill
malheureusement unfortunately
manche (m.) handle
Manche (f.) Channel
manger to eat
marché (m.) market
marcher to walk; to work (of machines)
mardi Tuesday
mari (m.) husband
marié married
marque (f.) brand
marron brown
match (m.) match
  m. de football football match
matin (m.) morning
médecin (m.) doctor
meilleur better
melon (m.) melon
menu (m.) set menu
mer (f.) sea
merci thank you
mercredi Wednesday
mère (f.) mother
métro (m.) underground
mettre to put
  j'ai mis I put
midi midday
mille thousand
minuit midnight
mœurs (f.pl.) customs
moi me
  pour m. for me
moins less
mois (m.) month
moment (m.) moment
  en ce m. at the moment
mon, ma, mes my
moniteur, -trice (f.) instructor
  m. de ski ski instructor
monnaie (f.) (small) change
monsieur (m.) gentleman

montagne (f.) mountain
monter to go up
montre (f.) watch
montrer to show
morceau (m.) piece
mûr ripe
musée (m.) museum

N
nager to swim
ne (verb) pas not
neiger to snow
n'est-ce pas? isn't it? (and other question tags)
nettoyer to clean
nez (m.) nose
Noël (m.) Christmas
noir black
nom (m.) name
non no
non-fumeurs non-smoking
notre, nos our
nouveau, nouvelle (f.) new
nuit (f.) night
numéro (m.) number

O
œil (m.), yeux (pl.) eye
œuf (m.) egg
offrir to offer
  j'ai offert I offered
Oh là là! Phew!
oignon (m.) onion
orange (f.) orange
ordonnance (f.) prescription
oreille (f.) ear
oreiller (m.) pillow
ou or
où where
  Où est . . . ? Where is . . . ?
  Où sont . . . ? Where are . . . ?
oublier to forget, leave
oui yes

P
pain (m.) bread
  petit p. bread roll

panne (f.) breakdown
  en p. broken down, out of order
pansement (m.) plaster, bandage
papeterie (f.) stationer's
papier (m.) paper
par by, per
  p. ici this way
parapluie (m.) umbrella
parce que because
Pardon! Excuse me!, I'm sorry!
pare-brise (m.) windscreen
parfait perfect
parfum (m.) perfume
parler to speak
particulier, -ière (f.) unusual, special
partir to depart, leave
  je pars I depart
  vous partez you depart
  je suis parti I departed
passeport (m.) passport
passer to pass
pastille (f.) lozenge
pâte (f.) dentifrice toothpaste
patinoire (f.) ice rink
pâtisserie (f.) pastry; cake shop
patte (f.) paw
payer to pay
pays (m.) country
paysage (m.) scenery
péage (m.) toll
pêche (f.) peach; fishing
penser to think
perdre to lose
  j'ai perdu I lost
permis (m.) de conduire driving licence
persil (m.) parsley
personne (f.) person
  ne (verb) p. no-one
  p. ne (verb) no-one
pétanque (f.) game of bowls
petit small
petits pois (m.pl.) peas
peu little
  un p. a little
peut-être perhaps
pharmacie (f.) chemist's

photo (f.) photograph
photographe (m. and f.) photographer
pièce (f.) piece; room
  3F la p. 3F each
pied (m.) foot
piscine (f.) swimming pool
piste (f.) ski run
  p. pour débutants nursery slope
place (f.) seat; square
plage (f.) beach
plaisir (m.) pleasure
plan (m.) plan, map
plateau (m.) tray, board (cheese)
plein full
  Le p. Fill up the tank
  en plein air outdoors, in the open air
pleuvoir to rain
  il pleut à verse it's raining heavily
plomb (m.) lead
  sans p. unleaded
plomber to fill (tooth)
plombier (m.) plumber
plus more
  p. cher que dearer than
plutôt rather
pneu (m.) tyre
poire (f.) pear
poireau (m.) leek
poisson (m.) fish
poivre (m.) pepper
police (f.) police
pomme (f.) apple
  p. de terre potato
populaire popular
porte (f.) door, gate
porto (m.) port (drink)
poste (m.) job; set (TV)
poste (f.) post office
pour for
  p. demain by tomorrow
  p. moi for me
pourquoi why
Pourriez-vous . . . ? Could you . . . ?
Pourrions-nous . . . ? Could we . . . ?
pouvoir to be able
  je peux I can
  vous pouvez you can

préférer to prefer
premier, -ière (f.) first
prendre to take
  je prends I take
  vous prenez you take
  j'ai pris I took
préparer to prepare
près de near
pression (f.) pressure
prêt ready
printemps (m.) spring
prix (m.) price
probablement probably
problème (m.) problem
  Pas de p.! No problem!
prochain next
  le mois p. next month
professeur (m.) teacher
profession (f.) profession
promenade (f.) walk; ride
  faire une p. to take a walk
prudent wise
prune (f.) plum
pruneau (m.) prune

Q
qualité (f.) quality
quand when
quel(s), quelle(s) (f.) which, what
quelque chose something
Qu'est-ce que . . . ? What . . . ?
question (f.) question
qui who, which

R
radiateur (m.) radiator
radio (f.) radio
raisin (m.) grape
raison (f.) reason
  avoir r. to be right
rapide fast
récemment recently
recevoir to receive
  j'ai reçu I received
recommander to recommend
récompense (f.) reward
regarder to look (at)

regretter to regret, be sorry
régulièrement regularly
remontée (f.) mécanique ski lift
remplir to fill
rendez-vous (m.) appointment
réserver to reserve, book
restaurant (m.) restaurant
rester to remain, stay
  je suis resté(e) I remained, stayed
rhume (m.) cold
rien nothing
  ne (verb) rien nothing
  rien ne (verb) nothing
  rien du tout nothing at all
robe (f.) dress
  r. de chambre dressing gown
romain Roman
rose pink
route (f.) road
rue (f.) street
ruines (f.pl.) ruins

S
sac (m.) bag
  s. de voyage travel bag
saison (f.) season
salle (f.) room
  s. de bains bathroom
  s. de séjour living room
samedi Saturday
sans without
santé (f.) health
saumon (m.) salmon
savoir to know (a fact)
  je sais I know
  vous savez you know
savon (m.) soap
secrétaire (m. and f.) secretary
sécurité (f.) safety
  en s. safe
séjour (m.) stay
sel (m.) salt
semaine (f.) week
serviette (f.) napkin, towel; briefcase
servir to serve
  je sers I serve
  vous servez you serve

seulement only
si if; emphatic yes
siècle (m.) century
siège (m.) seat
signer to sign
s'il vous plaît please
ski (m.) skiing
  s. alpin downhill skiing
  s. de fond cross-country skiing
  faire du s. to go skiing
soif (f.) thirst
  avoir soif to be thirsty
soir (m.) evening
soirée (f.) evening
soleil (m.) sun
son, sa, ses his/her/its
soucoupe (f.) saucer
soulager to soothe, relieve
soupe (f.) soup
sous under
sports (m.) nautiques water sports
station(f.)-service petrol station
station (f.) de sports d'hiver winter
  sports resort
sucre (m.) sugar
supermarché (m.) supermarket
supplément (m.) supplement
  en s. extra
supplémentaire additional
sur on
sûr sure
  Bien s.! Of course!
surtout especially
syndicat (m.) d'initiative tourist
  information office

T
table (f.) table
tableau (m.) picture, painting
tarte (f.) tart
  t. aux pommes apple tart
taux (m.) de change exchange rate
télécabine (f.) gondola lift
téléphérique (m.) cablecar
téléphoner to telephone
télésiège (m.) chairlift
téléski (m.) draglift

température (f.) temperature
temporairement temporarily
temps (m.) time; weather
  Quel t. fait-il? What's the weather
    like?
terrasse (f.) patio, terrace
terrain (m.) de camping campsite
terrine (f.) pâté
thé (m.) tea
  t. au citron lemon tea
théâtre (m.) theatre
thon (m.) tuna
timbre (m.) stamp
toilettes (f.pl.) toilet
tomate (f.) tomato
tort (m.) wrong
  avoir t. to be wrong
tour (f.) tower
  la t. Eiffel the Eiffel Tower
tour (m.) stroll; turn
tourisme (m.) tourism
tournedos (m.) fillet steak
tourner to turn
tout everything, all
  t. droit straight on
toux (f.) cough
train (m.) train
traîneau (m.) sleigh
très very
trop too, too much, too many
trou (m.) hole
trouver to find
truite (f.) trout
tube (m.) tube
  t. de dentifrice tube of toothpaste

U
urgent urgent
utiliser to use

V
vacances (f.pl.) holidays
valise (f.) suitcase
vallée (f.) valley
vendre to sell
  je vends I sell
  vous vendez you sell
  j'ai vendu I sold

vendredi Friday
venir to come
  je viens I come
  vous venez you come
  je suis venu(e) I came
vent (m.) wind
ventre (m.) stomach
vérifier to check
verre (m.) glass
vert green
viande (f.) meat
vide empty
vif, vive (f.) acute
village (m.) village
ville (f.) town
vin (m.) wine
  v. blanc white wine
  v. rouge red wine
visiter to visit
vite quickly
  le plus v. possible as quickly as
    possible
voici here is/are
voilà there is/are
voir to see
  j'ai vu I saw
voiture (f.) car
vol (m.) flight
voler to fly; to steal
votre, vos your
vouloir to want
  je voudrais I would like
  Voulez-vous . . . ? Would you . . . ?
voyage (m.) journey
vrai true
vue (f.) view

W
week-end (m.) weekend
whisky (m.) whisky

Y
yeux (m.pl.) eyes

Z
zéro zero

ENGLISH-FRENCH

A

able, to be a. pouvoir (see "can")
about (approximately) environ
accept, to accepter
ache
   my head aches j'ai mal à la tête
actor acteur (m.), actrice (f.)
additional supplémentaire
address adresse (f.)
admitted admis
aeroplane avion (m.)
affectionate affectueux
after après
afternoon après-midi (m. or f.)
   Good afternoon! Bonjour!
afterwards ensuite
against contre
ago il y a
   three days ago il y a trois jours
air air (m.)
   in the open air en plein air
airport aéroport (m.)
allow, to admettre
allowed admis
also aussi
ambulance ambulance (f.)
American américain
angry en colère
ankle cheville (f.)
aperitive apéritif (m.)
apple pomme (f.)
apply, to appliquer
appointment rendez-vous (m.)
   to arrange an a. fixer un rendez-vous
approach, to approcher
arm bras (m.)
around environ
arrive, to arriver
   I arrived je suis arrivé(e)
ask (for), to demander
at à
attach, to attacher
autumn automne (m.)

avoid, to éviter

B

bad mauvais
badly mal
bag sac (m.)
   travel b. sac de voyage
baker boulanger (m.)
baker's boulangerie (f.)
bank banque (f.)
   b.note billet (de banque)
barbecue barbecue (m.)
bathroom salle (f.) de bains
be,to être
   I am je suis
   you are vous êtes
   we are nous sommes
   I was j'étais
beach plage (f.)
beautiful beau, belle (f.)
because parce que
bed lit (m.)
bedroom chambre (f.)
been été
   he has b. il a été
beetroot betterave (f.)
begin, to commencer
behind derrière
believe, to croire
   I b. je crois
   you b. vous croyez
belt ceinture (f.)
better meilleur
between entre
bicycle bicyclette (f.)
big grand
bill addition (f.)
birthday anniversaire (m.)
blanket couverture (f.)
black noir
blue bleu
boarding pass carte (f.) d'embarquement

boat bateau (m.)
  cruise b. bateau-mouche
body corps (m.)
book livre (m.)
  b. shop librairie (f.)
bottle bouteille (f.)
bowls
  game of b. pétanque (f.)
box boîte (f.)
brand marque (f.)
bread pain (m.)
  French stick baguette (f.)
break, to casser
breakdown panne (f.)
  broken down en panne
breakfast petit déjeuner (m.)
  Is b. included? Le petit déjeuner est
    compris?
briefcase serviette (f.)
bring, to apporter
  to b. down descendre
  to b. up monter
brown marron
bun brioche (f.)
business affaires (f.pl.)
  on b. pour affaires
but mais
butcher's boucherie (f.)
buy, to acheter
by par
  b. tomorrow pour demain

C

cabbage chou (m.)
cable car téléphérique (m.)
call, to appeler
called, to be s'appeler
  I am called . . . je m'appelle . . .
camera appareil-photo (m.)
campsite terrain (m.) de camping
can
  I can je peux
  you can vous pouvez
  we can nous pouvons
car voiture (f.)
  c. registration document carte (f.)
    grise

card carte (f.)
Careful! Attention!
carrot carotte (f.)
case cas (m.)
  in that case dans ce cas-là
cashdesk caisse (f.)
castle château (m.)
cat chat (m.)
catch, to attraper
cathedral cathédrale (f.)
cauliflower chou-fleur (m.)
century siècle (m.)
certainly certainement
chairlift télésiège (m.)
change, to changer
Channel la Manche (f.)
cheap bon marché
check, to vérifier
cheese fromage (m.)
chemist's pharmacie (f.)
cheque chèque (m.)
  traveller's cheque chèque de voyage
cherry cerise (f.)
child enfant (m. and f.)
choose, to choisir
  I chose j'ai choisi
church église (f.)
cigarette cigarette (f.)
cinema cinéma (m.)
clean, to nettoyer
closed fermé
coach autocar, car (m.)
cod (fresh) cabillaud (m.)
coffee café (m.)
  white c. café au lait, café-crème
cold froid
  it's cold il fait froid
  to be cold avoir froid
cold rhume (m.)
colour couleur (f.)
  What colour? De quelle couleur?
come, to venir
  I come je viens
  you come vous venez
  I came je suis venu(e)
competition concours (m.)
constipated constipé

contact, to contacter
contents contenu (m.)
cooking cuisine (f.)
correct
   That's correct C'est ça
cough toux (f.)
Could you . . . ? Pourriez-vous . . . ?
Could we . . . ? Pourrions-nous . . . ?
country pays (m.)
countryside campagne (f.)
cow vache (f.)
cream crème (f.)
   anti-mosquito c. crème anti-
      moustiques
credit card carte (f.) de crédit
crown couronne (f.)
customer client, -e (f.)
customs mœurs (f.pl.)

D

dance bal (m.)
dance, to danser
dangerous dangereux, -se (f.)
daughter fille (f.)
day jour (m.), journée (f.)
dear cher, chère (f.)
deckchair chaise (f.) longue
delicious délicieux, -se (f.)
demand, to exiger
dentist dentiste (m. and f.)
deposit caution (f.)
describe, to décrire
dessert dessert (m.)
develop, to développer
   to have developed faire développer
diarrhoea diarrhée (f.)
different différent
disappear, to disparaître
   it has disappeared il/elle a disparu
divorced divorcé
do, to faire
   I do je fais
   you do vous faites
   we do nous faisons
   I did j'ai fait
doctor médecin (m.)
dog chien (m.)

door porte (f.)
double room chambre (f.) pour deux
      personnes
draglift téléski (m.)
dreadful affreux, -se (f.)
dress robe (f.)
dressing gown robe (f.) de chambre
drink boisson (f.)
drink, to boire
   I drink je bois
   you drink vous buvez
   we drink nous buvons
   I drank j'ai bu
driving licence permis (m.) de conduire
drop goutte (f.)
   ear drops gouttes pour les oreilles
   eye drops gouttes pour les yeux
duck canard (m.)
dustbin poubelle (f.)

E

ear oreille (f.)
eat, to manger
egg œuf (m.)
empty vide
engineer ingénieur (m.)
English anglais
enlarge, to agrandir
enough assez
enter, to entrer
entertainment distractions (f.pl.)
equipped équipé
escape
   to have a narrow escape l'échapper
      belle
especially surtout
evening soir (m.), soirée (f.)
   Good evening! Bonsoir!
everything tout
exception exception (f.)
exchange rate taux (m.) de change
excursion excursion (f.)
Excuse me! Excusez-moi!, Pardon!
expensive cher, chère (f.)
extra en supplément, supplémentaire
extremely extrêmement
eye œil (m.), yeux (pl.)

F

fairly assez
far loin
farm ferme (f.)
fast rapide
fasten, to attacher
father père (m.)
fax fax (m.)
festival fête (f.)
fill, to remplir
   to fill a tooth plomber une dent
   Fill it up (with petrol) Le plein
film (cinema) film (m.)
film (camera) pellicule (f.)
find, to trouver
Fine! Bien!
fireworks feu (m.) d'artifice
first premier, -ière (f.)
   first of all d'abord
first-aid plaster pansement (m.)
     (adhésif)
fish poisson (m.)
flight vol (m.)
flower fleur (f.)
fog brouillard (m.)
foot pied (m.)
for pour
   for me pour moi
forget, to oublier
fortunately heureusement
frankly franchement
free libre
free (of charge) gratuit
French français
fresh frais, fraîche (f.)
Friday vendredi
from de
front
   in f. of devant
full plein

G

garden jardin (m.)
garlic ail (m.)
gate porte (f.)
generally généralement
gentleman monsieur (m.)

German allemand
give, to donner
glass verre (m.)
glasses (spectacles) lunettes (f.pl.)
go, to aller
   I go je vais
   you go vous allez
   we go nous allons
   I went je suis allé(e)
   to go down descendre
   to go in entrer
   to go off partir
   to go out sortir
   to go up monter
gondola lift télécabine (f.)
good bon, bonne (f.)
   Good heavens! Mon Dieu!
Goodbye! Au revoir!
grape raisin (m.)
graze écorchure (f.)
green vert
grey gris
grill, to griller
grocer's épicerie (f.)
guide guide (m.)

H

handle manche (m.)
hard dur
hat chapeau (m.)
have, to avoir
   I have j'ai
   you have vous avez
   we have nous avons
   I had j'avais
have to, to devoir
   I must je dois
   you must vous devez
   we must nous devons
health santé (f.)
help, to aider
Help! Au secours!
hen poule (f.)
her son (m.), sa (f.), ses (pl.)
here ici
   Here is/are Voici, Voilà
hire, to louer

his son (m.), sa (f.), ses (pl.)
hit, to frapper
hole trou (m.)
holidays vacances (f.pl.)
horse cheval (m.)
hotel hôtel (m.)
hour heure (f.)
house maison (f.)
hovercraft aéroglisseur (m.)
how comment
   How are you? Comment allez-vous?
   How long? Combien de temps?
   How much?/How many? Combien?
   How much does that come to? Ça
     fait combien?
huge énorme
hundred cent
hungry, to be avoir faim
hurt, to
   My foot hurts J'ai mal au pied
husband mari (m.)

I
ice glace (f.)
ice cream glace (f.)
ice rink patinoire (f.)
ill malade
immediately immédiatement, tout de
   suite
important important
in dans
included compris
   Is service included? Le service est
     compris?
inside dedans
instructor moniteur (m.), monitrice (f.)
   ski i. moniteur/trice de ski
insurance assurance (f.)
interest, to intéresser
interesting intéressant
invite, to inviter
Irish irlandais
isn't it? (and other question tags) n'est-
   ce pas?
Italian italien, -enne (f.)
its son (m.), sa (f.), ses (pl.)

J
Japanese japonais
job poste (m.), emploi (m.)
journalist journaliste (m. and f.)
journey voyage (m.)
juicy juteux, -euse (f.)

K
keep, to garder
key clé (f.)
kitchen cuisine (f.)
know, to (person, place) connaître
   I know je connais
   you know vous connaissez
   we know nous connaissons
know, to (a fact) savoir
   I know je sais
   you know vous savez
   we know nous savons

L
lady dame (f.)
lake lac (m.)
landscape paysage (m.)
large grand
last dernier, -ière (f.)
laxative laxatif (m.)
   mild l. laxatif léger
learn, to apprendre
   I learn j'apprends
   you learn vous apprenez
   we learn nous apprenons
   I learnt j'ai appris
leave, to laisser
   (depart) partir
   (forget) oublier
lecture conférence (f.)
leek poireau (m.)
left
   on the left à gauche
less moins
lesson leçon (f.)
   skiing lessons leçons de ski
letter lettre (f.)
lettuce salade (f.), laitue (f.)
librarian bibliothécaire (m. and f.)
library bibliothèque (f.)

lift ascenseur (m.)
light léger, légère (f.)
like comme
   like that comme ça
like, to aimer
   I would like je voudrais
little peu
   a little un peu
live, to habiter
living room salle (f.) de séjour
local local
London Londres
long long, longue (f.)
   a long time longtemps
look (at), to regarder
look for, to chercher
look out onto, to donner sur
lose, to perdre
   I lost j'ai perdu
lost property office bureau (m.) des objets trouvés
lots, a lot beaucoup
   a lot of beaucoup de
love, to aimer
lovely beau, belle (f.)
lozenge pastille (f.)
luck chance (f.)
   Good luck! Bonne chance!
luggage bagages (m.pl.)
   hand l. bagages à main
lunch déjeuner (m.)

M
make, to faire
   I make je fais
   you make vous faites
   we make nous faisons
   I made j'ai fait
map plan (m.), carte (f.)
   road map carte routière
   street map plan de la ville
market marché (m.)
married marié(e)
match allumette (f.)
match match (m.)
   football m. match de football
matter, to

It doesn't matter Ça ne fait rien
It has no importance Ça n'a pas d'importance
me moi
   for me pour moi
meat viande (f.)
melon melon (m.)
menu carte (f.)
   set menu menu (m.)
midday midi
midnight minuit
milk lait (m.)
mistake erreur (f.)
moment moment (m.), instant (m.)
   at the m. en ce moment
   Just one m., please Un instant, s'il vous plaît
Monday lundi
money argent (m.)
month mois (m.)
more plus
   m. expensive than plus cher que
morning matin (m.)
   Good morning! Bonjour!
mother mère (f.)
mountain montagne (f.)
much beaucoup
museum musée (m.)
mushroom champignon (m.)
must, see "have to"
   We must leave Nous devons partir, Il faut partir
my mon (m.), ma (f.), mes (pl.)

N
name nom (m.)
   My name is . . . Je m'appelle . . .
narrow étroit
   to have a narrow escape l'échapper belle
near près de
need, to avoir besoin de
new (different) nouveau, nouvelle (f.)
new (brand-new) neuf, neuve (f.)
newspaper journal (m.), journaux (pl.)
next prochain
   n. week la semaine prochaine

next to à côté de
night nuit (f.)
   Goodnight! Bonne nuit!
no non
non-smoking non-fumeurs
noon midi
no-one personne
   I know no-one je ne connais
     personne
nose nez (m.)
not ne (verb) pas
   I do not smoke je ne fume pas
nothing rien
   I have nothing je n'ai rien
   nothing at all rien du tout
now maintenant
number numéro (m.)
   telephone n. numéro de téléphone
nursery slope piste (f.) pour débutants

O
o'clock
   five o'clock cinq heures
of de
Of course! Bien sûr!
offer, to offrir
   I offered j'ai offert
office bureau (m.)
   lost property o. bureau des objets
     trouvés
officer (police) agent (m.) de police
   Yes, Officer Oui, monsieur l'agent
oil huile (f.)
OK (I agree) D'accord
old ancien, -ienne (f.), vieux, vieille (f.)
olive olive (f.)
on sur
onion oignon (m.)
only seulement
open ouvert
opposite en face (de)
orange orange (f.)
   orange juice jus (m.) d'orange
other autre
our notre, nos
out of order en panne
over there là-bas

P
pain douleur (f.)
paper papier (m.)
parent parent (m.)
parsley persil (m.)
pass, to passer
passport passeport (m.)
pastry pâtisserie (f.)
patio terrasse (f.)
paw patte (f.)
pay, to payer
peach pêche (f.)
pear poire (f.)
peas petits pois (m.pl.)
pepper poivre (m.)
per par
   per night par nuit
perfect parfait
perfume parfum (m.)
perhaps peut-être
person personne (f.)
petrol essence (f.)
   p. station station(f.)-service
Phew! Oh là là!
photo photo (f.)
   to take a p. prendre une photo
photographer photographe (m. and f.)
picture (general) image (f.)
picture (painting) tableau (m.)
piece morceau (m.)
pillow oreiller (m.)
pillowcase taie (f.) d'oreiller
pink rose
plaster (first-aid) pansement (m.)
   adhésif
play, to jouer
   play tennis jouer au tennis
pleasant agréable
please s'il vous plaît
pleased content
pleasure plaisir (m.)
plum prune (f.)
plumber plombier (m.)
police police (f.)
   p. officer agent (m.) de police
   p. station commissariat (m.) de
     police

popular populaire
port (harbour) port (m.)
port (wine) porto (m.)
postcard carte (f.) postale
post office poste (f.), bureau (m.) de poste
potato pomme (f.) de terre
pound livre (f.)
prefer, to préférer
prepare, to préparer
prescription ordonnance (f.)
pressure pression (f.)
price prix (m.)
probably probablement
problem problème (m.)
  No problem! Pas de problème!
procession défilé (m.)
profession profession (f.)
prune pruneau (m.)
put, to mettre
  I put je mets
  you put vous mettez
  we put nous mettons
  I have put j'ai mis

Q
quality qualité (f.)
question question (f.)
  to ask a q. poser une question
quickly vite
quite, fairly assez

R
rabbit lapin (m.)
radiator radiateur (m.)
radio radio (f.)
rain, to pleuvoir
  It's raining Il pleut
  It's raining heavily Il pleut à verse
rather plutôt
ready prêt
receive, to recevoir
  I received j'ai reçu
regularly régulièrement
remain, to rester
  I remained je suis resté(e)
remainder reste (m.)

reserve, to réserver
rest, to se reposer
restaurant restaurant (m.)
reward récompense (f.)
right
  on the r. à droite
  That's r. C'est ça
  to be right avoir raison
ripe mûr
road route (f.)
  road map carte (f.) routière
roll (bread) petit pain (m.)
Roman romain
room (general) pièce (f.)
  bedroom chambre (f.)
  living room salle (f.) de séjour
ruins ruines (f.pl.)
Russian russe

S
safe en sécurité
salad salade (f.)
salmon saumon (m.)
salt sel (m.)
Saturday samedi
saucer soucoupe (f.)
scenery paysage (m.)
Scottish écossais
scratch égratignure (f.)
sea mer (f.)
season saison (f.)
seat siège (m.), place (f.)
secretary secrétaire (m. and f.)
see, to voir
  I see je vois
  you see vous voyez
  we see nous voyons
  I saw j'ai vu
sell, to vendre
  I sell je vends
  you sell vous vendez
  we sell nous vendons
  I sold j'ai vendu
send, to envoyer
serious grave
serve, to servir
  I serve je sers

you serve vous servez
we serve nous servons
I served j'ai servi
serviette serviette (f.)
set menu menu (m.)
sheep mouton (m.)
sheet drap (m.)
shirt chemise (f.)
shoe chaussure (f.)
shop (large) magasin (m.)
shop (small) boutique (f.)
shopping courses (f.pl.)
   to do one's shopping faire ses
     courses
short court
show, to montrer
shower douche (f.)
side côté (m.)
sign, to signer
since (time) depuis
since (reason) puisque
sing, to chanter
single person célibataire (m. and f.)
single room chambre (f.) pour une
     personne
ski ski (m.)
   to ski skier, faire du ski
   s. boots chaussures (f.pl.) de ski
   s. lift remontée (f.) mécanique
   s. pass forfait(m.)-skieur
   s. run piste (f.)
skiing ski (m.)
   cross-country s. ski de fond
   downhill s. ski alpin
sleigh traîneau (m.)
slide (photo) diapositive (f.)
slow lent
slowly lentement
small petit
smoke, to fumer
smoking, non-smoking fumeurs, non-
     fumeurs
snooze somme (m.)
snow, to neiger
snowfall chute (f.) de neige
so donc
soap savon (m.)

some du, de la, de l', des
something quelque chose
son fils (m.)
soothe, to soulager
sorry, to be regretter
   I'm sorry Excusez-moi, Pardon
soup soupe (f.)
Spanish espagnol
speak, to parler
sport sport (m.)
   water sports sports nautiques
spring (season) printemps (m.)
square (in town) place (f.)
stamp timbre (m.)
star étoile (f.)
start, to commencer
station (rail) gare (f.)
station (underground) station (f.)
stationer's papeterie (f.)
stay séjour (m.)
stay, to rester
steak bifteck (m.)
   fillet s. tournedos (m.)
steal, to voler
stomach estomac (m.), ventre (m.)
   upset s. estomac dérangé
straight on tout droit
strawberry fraise (f.)
street rue (f.)
   street map plan (m.) de la ville
strong fort
sugar sucre (m.)
suitcase valise (f.)
sum somme (f.)
summer été (m.)
sun soleil (m.)
sunburn coup (m.) de soleil
   to get s. attraper des coups de soleil
Sunday dimanche
sunglasses lunettes (f.pl.) de soleil
sunshade parasol (m.)
supermarket supermarché (m.)
supplement supplément (m.)
sure sûr
swallow, to avaler
swim, to nager
swimming pool piscine (f.)

T

table table (f.)
tablet comprimé (m.)
take, to prendre
  I take je prends
  you take vous prenez
  we take nous prenons
  I took j'ai pris
tart tarte (f.)
  apple t. tarte aux pommes
taste goût (m.)
taste, to goûter
tea thé (m.)
  lemon t. thé au citron
teacher professeur (m.)
telephone téléphone (m.)
telephone, to téléphoner (à)
temperature température (f.)
thank you merci
that ça
  like that comme ça
theatre théâtre (m.)
them les
  with them avec eux/elles (f.)
there là
there is/are il y a
therefore donc
these ces
think, to penser
thirsty, to be avoir soif
this ce, cette
thousand mille
throat gorge (f.)
  I have a sore throat J'ai mal à la
    gorge
Thursday jeudi
ticket billet (m.)
time temps (m.)
  at what time? à quelle heure?
  What time is it? Quelle heure est-il?
tin (can) boîte (f.)
to à
tobacconist's bureau (m.) de tabac
today aujourd'hui
toilet toilettes (f.pl.)
toll péage (m.)
tomato tomate (f.)

tomorrow demain
too, too much trop
tooth dent (f.)
toothpaste pâte (f.) dentifrice
tourism tourisme (m.)
tourist touriste (m. and f.)
tourist information office syndicat (m.)
    d'initiative
towel serviette (f.)
tower tour (f.)
  the Eiffel Tower la tour Eiffel
town ville (f.)
town hall mairie (f.)
train train (m.)
travel, to voyager
traveller's cheque chèque (m.) de
    voyage
tree arbre (m.)
trout truite (f.)
true vrai
  It's true C'est vrai
tube tube (m.)
  t. of toothpaste tube de dentifrice
tube (underground) métro (m.)
turn, to tourner
Tuesday mardi
tuna thon (m.)
tyre pneu (m.)

U

umbrella parapluie (m.)
unbearable insupportable
under sous
underground métro (m.)
understand comprendre
  I understand je comprends
  you understand vous comprenez
  we understand nous comprenons
  I understood j'ai compris
unemployed au chômage
unemployment chômage (m.)
unfortunately malheureusement
unleaded sans plomb
upset, to déranger
urgent urgent
use, to utiliser

V

vacuum cleaner aspirateur (m.)
valley vallée (f.)
vanity case vanity-case (m.)
vegetable légume (m.)
very très
view vue (f.)
village village (m.)
visit, to visiter

W

wait (for), to attendre
  I wait j'attends
  you wait vous attendez
  we wait nous attendons
  I waited j'ai attendu
walk promenade (f.)
  to go for a w. faire une promenade
walk, to marcher
want, to vouloir, désirer
  I want je veux
  you want vous voulez
  we want nous voulons
warm chaud
  It's warm Il fait chaud
  to be warm avoir chaud
washing powder lessive (f.)
watch montre (f.)
watch, to regarder
water eau (f.)
  mineral w. eau minérale
  w. sports sports (m.) nautiques
way
  this way par ici
weather temps (m.)
  What's the weather like? Quel temps fait-il?
Wednesday mercredi
week semaine (f.)
weekend week-end (m.)
Welcome . . . ! Bienvenue . . . !
well bien
Welsh gallois
what . . . ? qu'est-ce que . . . ?
  What are you buying? Qu'est-ce que vous achetez?
when quand

where où
  Where is . . . ?, Where are . . . ? Où est . . . ?, Où sont . . . ?
which, what quel(s) (m.), quelle(s) (f.)
whisky whisky (m.)
white blanc, blanche (f.)
why pourquoi
wife femme (f.)
wind vent (m.)
windscreen pare-brise (m.)
wine vin (m.)
  red w. vin rouge
  white w. vin blanc
winter hiver (m.)
  w. sports resort station (f.) de sports d'hiver
wise prudent
wish, to désirer
with avec
without sans
wonderful magnifique
Would you . . . ? Voulez-vous . . . ?
work, to (general) travailler
work, to (of machines) marcher
write, to écrire
  I write j'écris
  you write vous écrivez
  we write nous écrivons
  I wrote j'ai écrit
  Will you write it down? Voulez-vous l'écrire?
wrong faux, fausse (f.)
  That's wrong C'est faux
  to be wrong avoir tort

Y

year an (m.), année (f.)
yellow jaune
yes oui
yesterday hier
your votre, vos

Z

zero zéro

Index

127

Trouvé
CHAT BLANC avec patte noire, très affectueux, s'appelle César. Tel 87.65.43.21

Of course, the presence of Caesar the cat, in some chapters of this course, was purely for fun. In reality animals should not be taken abroad because of the period of quarantine required on return to the UK.